THE UNITED STATES
AND THE
ATLANTIC COMMUNITY

THE UNITED STATES AND THE ATLANTIC COMMUNITY
Issues and Prospects

A Series of Public Lectures Held at
The University of Texas, Spring, 1966

Edited by JAMES R. ROACH, Director of Special Programs,
College of Arts and Sciences, The University of Texas

Introduction by M. DONALD HANCOCK,
Department of Government, The University of Texas

UNIVERSITY OF TEXAS PRESS   AUSTIN & LONDON

Library of Congress Catalog Card No. 67–27782

Copyright © 1967 by the University of Texas Press
All Rights Reserved

First Published in *The Texas Quarterly*
Volume IX, Number 3 (Fall 1966)
Copyright © 1966 by *The Texas Quarterly*

Printed in the United States of America

LIBRARY
FLORIDA STATE UNIVERSITY
TALLAHASSEE, FLORIDA

CONTENTS

Atlantic Agenda: An Introduction 3
    M. DONALD HANCOCK

NATO: Evolution or Decline 7
    HENRY A. KISSINGER

The Atlantic Economy: Partners and Rivals 19
    ANDRÉ PHILIP

Germany, the Continuing Challenge 33
    HANS SPEIER

Western Europe, Eastern Europe, and the Soviet Union 55
    FRITZ ERLER

American Interests and Europe's Future 69
    JOHN J. MCCLOY

BIOGRAPHICAL NOTES

JAMES R. ROACH is professor of government and Director of Special Programs at The University of Texas. He is widely recognized as an expert on Southeast Asia, and in 1966 was appointed by the President to serve as a member of the Board of Foreign Scholarships.

M. DONALD HANCOCK conducted the Atlantic Community Seminar. He is an assistant professor of government at The University of Texas.

HENRY A. KISSINGER is professor of government at Harvard University. At various times he has been a consultant to the National Security Council, the Arms Control and Disarmament Agency, and the Weapons Systems Evaluation Group of the Joint Chiefs of Staff. His books include *Nuclear Weapons and Foreign Policy* (1958), *The Necessity for Choice* (1961), and *The Troubled Partnership: A Reappraisal of the Western Alliance* (1965).

ANDRÉ PHILIP, now a professor of economics at the Sorbonne, has a public career tracing back to membership in the French Chamber of Deputies in 1936. He was active in the French underground during World War II and then became a minister in General de Gaulle's Free French Government in Exile. Later posts included those of Minister of Finance and Minister of the National Economy. Among his publications is *United Europe and Its Place in International Trade*.

HANS SPEIER has been affiliated with the RAND Corporation since 1948. An authority on postwar German politics, he emigrated to the United States in 1933, taught sociology at the New School for Social Research in New York, and in 1948 was appointed chief of the social science division at RAND, becoming a member of its Research Council in 1960. Dr. Speier is the author of *Order and the Risk of War* (1952), *German Rearmament and Atomic War* (1957), and *Divided Berlin* (1961).

FRITZ ERLER, the late foreign policy expert in the "shadow" Social Democratic cabinet of the Federal Republic of Germany, was closely associated with the European integration movement. Before his death last February he was a member of the Consultative Assembly of the Council of Europe and of the Association of Western European Union. Among his publications is *Democracy in Germany* (1965), based on a series of lectures delivered at Harvard University in 1964.

JOHN J. MCCLOY is a member of the New York law firm of Milbank, Tweed, Hadley and McCloy, is a former Chairman of the Board of the Chase Manhattan Bank, and is recently retired as Chairman of the Ford Foundation. His record of public service includes: Assistant Secretary of War (1941–45), president of the World Bank (1947–49), and U.S. Military Governor and High Commissioner for Germany (1949–52). He was co-ordinator of the United States government disarmament activities from 1961–63.

THE UNITED STATES
AND THE
ATLANTIC COMMUNITY

Atlantic Agenda: An Introduction

M. DONALD HANCOCK

As much of the world seethed in ferment—from the Dominican Republic to Vietnam—the relative quiescence of North Atlantic relations seemed to offer a welcome contrast of stability. Today this calm is disrupted, and Western statesmen confront a grave crisis of confidence that threatens to undermine the efficacy of the Atlantic Community.

Because of the current reappraisal of the Atlantic Alliance, occasioned by President Charles de Gaulle's decision to end French participation in NATO's "integrated" military structure, the essays that follow assume timely significance. Presented at the University of Texas during the spring of 1966 as a series of public lectures entitled "The United States and the Atlantic Community: Issues and Prospects," the papers focus on specialized aspects of the Atlantic partnership. All of them reflect a common concern for the continued viability of the Alliance in its broadest political, economic, and strategic perspectives.

Any consideration of the present state and future prospects of the Atlantic Alliance must begin with a restatement of the historical assumptions underlying the cohesiveness of the North Atlantic area. The first is that the Soviet Union, together with its Eastern European allies, poses a serious military, ideological, and political threat to the West. Secondly, the United States and the nations of Western Europe are united in meeting this challenge by common interests of survival, shared cultural traditions, the promise of mutual economic benefits, and the desire to preserve Western influence in non-Atlantic regions.

Given this community of interests, the nations bordering on the North Atlantic and the Mediterranean achieved notable success during the first two decades after World War II in combining their resources in a common pursuit of peace and stability. The United States, Canada, and thirteen European states linked military forces through NATO in an effort to deter potential Soviet aggression. In cooperation with most of the remaining nations of Western Europe the NATO Allies have sought to strengthen their economic ties and to coordinate foreign aid policies within the framework of the Organization for Economic Cooperation and Development. The six members of the European Economic Community approach the culmination of the postwar integration movement with the creation of a single market, protected by a common external tariff, for the free movement of industrial goods, agricultural products, workers, and investments.

Several marked failures of communication, highlighted by the Suez debacle of

1956, produced significant strains within the Alliance during its years of maturation. Despite instances of Allied discord, however, the over-all balance sheet of Atlantic relations proved a propitious one.

Yet the future of the Atlantic Community is not so secure. Sustained economic growth and the success of the integration experiment have engendered a new mood of European assertiveness. De Gaulle's challenge to United States leadership and the principle of military coordination within NATO is but symptomatic of a growing European awareness that American hegemony in the North Atlantic area has come to an end. The Sino-Soviet conflict and the perceptible rise of polycentrism within the Eastern European Communist Commonwealth have diminished the overt threat of armed conflict in Central Europe and have opened new avenues for reappraising East-West relations. The tragic stalemate of German division has yielded to cautious feelers on both sides of the Elbe River to reëstablish contacts among political spokesmen. Whether these efforts will lead to a significant amelioration in the present antagonism between West and East Germany, at least in the foreseeable future, is debatable; but the point is that the Germans, like the French, are growing increasingly wary of perpetuating what has become for them a stagnating status quo.

The contributors to this series address themselves to the implications of these changes for the future of Atlantic relations. Implicit in each of their presentations is the premise that the United States cannot abdicate responsibility for guiding developments beyond the present. This does not suggest that American policymakers should attempt to dictate the future. It does mean that responsible government officials and concerned citizens, in earnest collaboration with their European counterparts, must confront the problems of the Atlantic area with as much honesty, courage, and imagination as they can muster. As André Philip correctly points out in his assessment of Atlantic trade policies, the sense of common purpose that seems to have dissipated among the North Atlantic partners in recent years can be restored—if at all—only after a frank exchange of views between American and European spokesmen. At the same time the success of such an undertaking, Professor Kissinger emphasizes, will depend on the capacity of Atlantic leaders to look beyond immediate crises to the ultimate goals they wish to achieve.

What feasible goals might serve as guidelines for reconstituting Atlantic relations on a more durable basis? In considering this question it is useful to distinguish between means of improving Allied communication and the ends of policy. Structural reforms within NATO would conceivably alleviate a major source of Allied dissonance, rooted in habitual American dominance of the Alliance, by according the Europeans greater influence in shaping Atlantic foreign policies. This might be accomplished, as Kissinger suggests, by creating a new executive committee to consider long-range Alliance objectives and over-all defense strategy. But innovations in

Atlantic Agenda: An Introduction 5

NATO's structure will be meaningful only if they are coupled with substantial progress toward resolving the issues that presently impede the evolution of the Atlantic Community beyond a mere holding operation.

Until Britain either joins the EEC or firmly renounces her potential interest in seeking membership the debate on the future form of European political union remains inconclusive. But until European leaders reach a consensus on political integration as a logical (though not inevitable) complement to the Common Market, there is little likelihood of realizing a more equal Atlantic partnership to supersede the present imbalance weighted to American advantage. In the meantime De Gaulle's demand for greater political and military autonomy within the framework of NATO serves only to delay the necessary reassessment of Western defense requirements in light of growing diversity within the Soviet bloc.

The suspended issue of German division poses an additional obstacle to further progress in strengthening Atlantic ties. As a matter of declaratory policy the NATO Allies continue to support the Federal Republic's claim to speak for the entire German nation and its aspirations to seek reunification on Western terms; but simultaneous efforts to pursue a *détente* with the Soviet Union have engendered recurrent German fears of possible Western concessions at Germany's expense. A potential ground swell of German dissatisfaction with Alliance policies, leading perhaps to an assertion of independence along the same course charted by France, would exert a profoundly negative effect on the already strained fabric of Atlantic relations.

A final theme of disunity, one not explicitly explored as a separate topic in these lectures, is the continuing crisis generated by the inability of Allied leaders to coordinate adequately their policies in non-Atlantic areas. The divisive impact of unilateral action outside the NATO region—such as American involvement in South Vietnam—suggests an urgent need to seek more intensive collaboration in formulating joint Atlantic policies toward the "third world."

These issues define the principal intermediate goals of the Atlantic Community. The single most important step in resolving them must be taken by the Europeans themselves in forging closer political ties, presumably through some form of confederation. Within such a framework European leaders could then engage American spokesmen as more equal partners in a joint quest for consensus in formulating Atlantic policies toward the Soviet bloc, non-Atlantic regions, and the question of German reunification. It is unrealistic to assume that all the divergent interests and conflicting attitudes within the Alliance can be reconciled in a single "grand design" of Atlantic partnership. But if the present crisis of confidence is to be overcome Atlantic leaders must begin now to explore means of reaching a minimum level of mutual responsiveness and renewed trust.

In long-range terms the United States should anticipate the gradual emancipation of Western Europe from the postwar pattern of American tutelage. As the threat of conflict in Central Europe continues to subside, thereby qualifying the necessity for common defense as a principal assumption sustaining the unity of the North Atlantic area, the United States will confront a Europe increasingly conscious of its own interests and powerful enough to pursue them in an independent fashion. The contemporary Alliance structure will no longer be justified in an era in which ambiguous factors, such as economic ties and shared cultural antecedents, have largely superseded the threat of possible aggression as the primary cohesive impulse within the Atlantic Community.

Thus as American and European leaders consider possible NATO reforms in light of the French withdrawal, they should simultaneously plan ahead for the liquidation of NATO within a reconstituted Atlantic Community. It is axiomatic that if the Europeans are able to unite politically they will rightfully assert their claim to an autonomous defense capacity unencumbered by American strategic priorities. Without renouncing its present military and political commitments on the Continent, at least until such unity is achieved, the United States must embark on the creative task of promoting European confidence and independence even at the risk of encouraging possible conflicts of interest between Western Europe and North America. Through positive accommodation to European autonomy the United States could thus prepare the way for a new synthesis of common endeavors in the Atlantic area based on complementary tiers of shared responsibility and leadership. The alternative response—American resistance to Europe's search for a new identity—will lead to continued stagnation and drift from one crisis to another.

NATO: Evolution or Decline

HENRY A. KISSINGER

Perhaps the most creative policy that the United States has pursued in the postwar period is the development of its Atlantic relationships. Through a series of farsighted measures the United States helped Europe to recover economically from World War II, assured its military security, and thus laid the groundwork for eventual European integration. It has been extremely painful, therefore, to many of those who deserve the greatest credit for developing existing relationships to find that today, only two decades later, some of these policies are being challenged within the Atlantic area.

In recent years the debate about the future of the Atlantic relationship has been intense, and has focused on the somewhat out-of-scale figure of President de Gaulle. Many people assume that the pattern of relationships that was established immediately after World War II would have continued but for the emergence of President de Gaulle. I should like to suggest that the problems we are facing in the Atlantic Alliance today are the inevitable consequence of the success of our previous policies. They are due to factors that could not be created by one man, and they will not end with the disappearance of that individual. It would be unusual if a policy devised in the late 1940s were still adequate in the 1960s; our challenge today stems not from the fact that our previous policies were wrong but from the fact that those policies have accomplished their purposes and that we need another leap of the imagination similar to the one that took place two decades ago.

In discussing the changing nature of these relationships I shall group them into two categories. Some factors are inherent in the structure of the contemporary international system. Others are amenable to changes of policy. Let me speak first about the fundamental factors that are not caused by acts of policy.

The most obvious and striking, of course, is the recovery of Europe. When the United States encountered Europe at the close of World War II, the end of our isolation coincided with the economic and military collapse of most European societies. Every European country, with the exception of Great Britain, had been destroyed during the war. Every country had been occupied at one stage or another. Europe's recovery depended on American economic, political, and military support. In such a situation it was natural that the United States should adopt a position of senior partner and that the Europeans should act more as lobbyists than as equals. European policy consisted of trying to influence decisions made in Washington; thus, during the immediate postwar period the country which was most successful in dealing with the United States was Great Britain, which had many unofficial contacts with the United States. But, as Europe recovered economically, largely with American assistance, its traditional political vigor returned to some extent. The pattern of relationship which was appropriate during a period of dependence was bound to alter when Europe was again in a position to express its own view of the world; and, as I shall point out later, I think it is in our interest, as well as in Europe's interest, that it be encouraged to express its own view of the world, rather than reflecting that of the United States.

Another factor that has changed relationships is the process of decolonization. In the 1940s and at an accelerated pace in the 1950s, several of our European allies were engaged in the process of either liquidating colonial empires or unsuccessfully (as it developed) attempting to hold on to their colonial empires. At that time we took the position that the greater interests of freedom required a measure of dissociation between us and the Europeans in areas outside of Europe. Now the process of decolonization has been essentially completed and the focus of interest of the European countries has shifted almost entirely to Europe. Indeed, in one of the ironic reversals of roles, we are now using the arguments of Europe of the 1950s, and the Europeans are answering us with the American script of that decade.

In the 1950s, our European allies were trying to convince us that the wars they were fighting in Indochina or in Algeria or in Africa were not merely colonial wars but involved greater concerns. In the 1960s, in different circumstances to be sure, we are trying to convince our European allies that they should assist us in Vietnam. However, whatever the merits of our arguments, the attitude of the Europeans toward our involvement in Vietnam is almost exactly the same as our attitude toward European problems until the outbreak of World War II. It is precisely because our European allies do not think that their primary interests are at stake in Vietnam that we are not going to be able to get from them any more than token support. There is now an inevitable difference in perspective between us and the Europeans on matters outside of Europe. We are now the only country in the West that is psychologically, physically, and economically capable of pursuing global responsibilities, and no amount of exhortation is going to change that fact.

A change in the perception of the Soviet threat since the first years of NATO has also altered European-American relationships. In the early period of the Atlantic Alliance our European allies were afraid that the Soviet Union might launch a military attack on Europe at almost any moment. They were prepared, therefore, to pay a heavy price for American military support. The memory of the period of American isolation was still so fresh that Europeans believed they had to purchase our support by subordinating their policy to ours. Since then, most Europeans, rightly or wrongly, have become convinced that the Soviet military threat has diminished, and that, even if a military threat still exists, the United States is irreversibly committed to Europe's defense. Many of the difficulties in NATO arise not from any French doubts about out commitment to defend Europe but rather from the fact that our commitment is so firm. De Gaulle is so sure of our support that he believes he risks nothing by pursuing, under the protective American umbrella, policies which are sometimes contrary to our wishes.

Another factor is the nature of modern technology. We live in a period in which it is possible to destroy any part of the globe from any other part of the globe in a matter of minutes. When NATO was founded the United States was immune from attack. Today, according to Secretary McNamara's published testimony, a nuclear war might kill as many as one hundred forty million Americans. It must make a difference to an American President whether he is confronted with the situation of 1945, when American territory was inviolate, or the current situation, where millions of Americans might be killed in a matter of hours—just as it must make a difference in the calculations of an aggressor. This does not mean that we will not carry out our commitment, but it does mean that the nature of commitments in the nuclear age has changed fundamentally. In the past a nation would carry out a pledge of an alliance because the consequences of failing to resist would be worse than the consequence of resistance. In other words, the fear was that a later war would have more serious consequences than would immediate commitment of oneself. In the nuclear age, this relationship does not inevitably hold: it is at least conceivable that circumstances might arise in which the worse eventuality might appear to be the outbreak of nuclear war.

As a result, some commitments become less credible, while those which remain credible become so firm that they are not basically affected by the actions of one's allies. This accounts for the fact that, in contemporary international relations, the actions of allies and neutrals tend to merge. A few years ago, after the Chinese attack on India in 1962, Prime Minister Nehru was asked if he had been mistaken in not making an alliance with the United States. Nehru replied, "Not at all," and went on to explain that had he made an alliance he would have had to purchase military equipment at going rates; by waiting until he was attacked, he received it at cost. When India was attacked, it received about the same assistance, even though it was neutral, that Pakistan would have received even though it was an ally. Similarly, President de Gaulle, even though he is an ally, is pursuing on many issues—Vietnam being a notable example—a policy which in the past was more appropriate to that of the neutral. In other words, the risks of nuclear war produce a curious situation in which neutrals receive the protection which used to be accorded allies, and in which allies have the privilege of conducting their own foreign policy—a privilege which used to be confined to neutrals.

In addition to these permanent factors, which seem to me not to be susceptible to policy decisions, a number of policy choices also have affected the relationships within the Atlantic area. The first has to do with the way in which a united Europe might best be organized and the direction that this Europe should take. President de Gaulle, on the one hand, holds the view that a united Europe should be built on the confederate principle. According to it the several states would remain. Whatever unity emerges would come out of an association of separate political units. The opposite point of view, held by Jean Monnet and his group, argues that a united Europe should come about on the model of the United States with federal institutions, supranational in character, that transcend the separate states. This debate has recently produced an inconclusive showdown over the issue of what kind of powers the Common Market Commissions should have.

Another issue concerns the kind of policy a united Europe should pursue. Some wish it to pursue a third-force policy between the United States and the Soviet Union, while others argue that it should be the other pillar of an Atlantic partnership.

Another policy disagreement concerns the nature of East-West relations. No issue in the Alliance, probably, has been more divisive than that resulting from attempts of various Western statesmen to try to demonstrate that they have the magic key for dealing with the Soviet leaders. Every time a separate approach to the Soviet leaders is made by any of the major countries of the Alliance, whether it is the United States, Great Britain, France, or the Federal Republic, all the other countries become disquieted and maneuver to protect themselves. In the 1950s this led to the situation in which President Eisenhower, after announcing that he was going to see Khrushchev, had to take a tour of Europe in order to reassure jittery allies of his good intentions. Some of President de Gaulle's actions reflect his conviction that sooner or later a Soviet-American understanding will come about and he wants either to be able to prevent it or to be in such a strong position that he at least cannot be ignored. One of the major problems that the Atlantic nations will have to solve is whether they will be able to talk to the Communist countries with one voice or whether they are going to continue to try separate approaches.

The question of German unity is another example. For twenty years after World War II German energies were concentrated on the problem of economic recovery, and on achieving a degree of equality within the Atlantic Alliance. German national policy cannot permanently accept, however, the division of the country and the fact that eighteen million Germans are under Communist rule. As Germany recovers economically and as it becomes an equal partner in the Atlantic Alliance the issue of national unity will become a more and more pronounced problem. In this we face

NATO: Evolution or Decline

a latent source of tension in the Alliance, because, while German unity is a matter of great importance to the Germans, no other ally—to put it mildly—feels the desire for German unity with equal intensity. Many allies can easily visualize a world in which Germany remains divided almost permanently. Yet if the Alliance does not support Germany in its desire for unification Germany is going to attempt to achieve unification in its own way.

Another range of issues has to do with the broad question of military security which was the initial basis of the Atlantic organization. In the 1950s the American strategic doctrine was based on the doctrine of massive retaliation. This meant, in case of an attack on Europe, that the United States would retaliate almost automatically against the Soviet homeland with nuclear weapons. On technical and military grounds this was not a very satisfactory strategic doctrine, because it forced the United States to run enormous risks in an automatic manner, and it deprived the President of freedom of decision. For our allies, however, who did not have the power of decision anyway, it offered a great degree of reassurance. The very "automaticity" of the United States response, which made some of us who were writing on strategic matters in the 1950s uneasy, gave the Europeans a sense of security.

In the 1960s the United States modified its strategic doctrine and replaced the doctrine of massive retaliation with the principles of flexible response. This means that we intend to tailor our response to the circumstances of the moment, according to decisions made by the President and the Secretary of Defense in view of the particular provocation we might confront. We have placed great stress on developing the maximum number of options for our military establishment. Each option is designed to give our political leadership the maximum freedom of decision. But this in turn has provoked a sharp dialogue between ourselves and many Europeans.

The very quality of flexibility that makes this military posture attractive to us makes it worrisome to our allies. We have tried to reserve to our political leaders freedom of choice for circumstances that cannot be defined ahead of time. Our allies in turn have sought reassurance in other ways: by participating in our planning, or in the possession of nuclear weapons, and, above all, by trying to make sure that the decisions made in Washington would not be unilateral. They are anxious that flexible response, as it is implemented, reflect the interests and concerns of all and not simply those of the American bureaucracy and American leadership. Ultimately, I suspect, we will have to make a choice between technical refinement and political reliability. If we want a truly flexible military response, we will have to concede autonomy in nuclear matters to the Europeans. If we do not want the Europeans to have autonomy in nuclear matters, then they must have a role in our political decision-making process which goes far beyond anything that has so far been envisaged.

Over the past two decades, as these differences have become more apparent, the

United States has continued to argue that a united Europe—united on the federal principle—could be a partner of the United States and could share our burdens around the world. We have consistently promoted what I described as the Jean Monnet view; in fact, we have sometimes promoted it more ardently than any European except Jean Monnet himself. The United States has insisted that the military defense of the Atlantic area is indivisible and has suggested a variety of schemes for achieving what we call central command and control over all the nuclear weapons in the Alliance. On the whole, the United States has been hostile to special groupings in the Atlantic Alliance—for example, the Franco-German treaty which, at least unofficially, we have sought to render inoperative. Many of our political spokesmen, especially those in the State Department, have taken a consistently dim view of President de Gaulle, and have attempted to isolate him through such measures as the proposed NATO multilateral force or by tying German military purchases to the United States.

Although the basic motivation of American policy was constructive, I would argue that in some respects we have tried to apply lessons drawn from the American experience somewhat too literally in circumstances where they are inappropriate.

When the United States established a federal union on the North American continent the states had emerged through similar experiences. They had gone through a war against a common enemy and were starting their careers with roughly similar resources and with a common background. In Europe the states emerged by quite different historical routes, and their sense of separate identity is much more highly developed. It is no accident that in Europe those states which advocate the supranational principle, on the whole, are the small countries like Belgium and Luxembourg, or the countries that were smashed in the war, like Germany and Italy. The old nations of Europe—France and Britain—have consistently opposed the principle of supranationality.

Secondly, I doubt that Europe, even if it unites on the supranational principle, will do so in order to share our world-wide commitments. The willingness to assume global responsibilities is not necessarily dependent upon the availability of resources. Before World War II the United States had the resources, but it was not prepared to assume even European, not to mention global, responsibilities. If Europe unites it will not be to share burdens designed in Washington, but to vindicate a different, or at least an autonomous, conception of international affairs.

Thirdly, I disagree with the devil theory of international politics. A senior official in Washington once said about De Gaulle, "How can one man stand up against two hundred and fifty million?" The answer to this is that of course one man could not stand up to two hundred and fifty million, and if one man does seem so to stand, it is because he reflects something deeper than a personal point of view. It is a great mistake to assume that one can predict the future of a political structure by listening to the pronouncements of political leaders who create it. Many people believe that a confederal Europe—because it is advocated by De Gaulle—is bound to be hostile to the United States, while a federal Europe—because it is advocated by such a great friend of the United States as Jean Monnet—is certain to be friendly toward the United States. I would venture the heretical thought that a confederal Europe may be easier for the United States to deal with than a unitary European state. When I imagine an election in Europe, involving voters from Scotland to Sicily and encompassing Schleswig-Holstein and Southern France, I try to visualize what kind of campaign could possibly achieve a common denominator in the face of such diversity. I would fear that a great premium would be put on demagoguery, and it seems very probable to me that in such circumstances a rather extreme form of nationalism might prove the only way to achieve a common identity. It is not at all clear what *American* interest is served by the passionate advocacy of *one* particular form of European unity.

I wonder, also, if it is wise to concentrate much attention on the very technical, complicated, and inherently insoluble problem of nuclear control. A succession of schemes have proposed a degree of nuclear sharing within the Atlantic Alliance. All of them seem to me to suffer from the disability that any discussion of the conduct of nuclear war is inherently divisive. No political leader, no matter how sincere, anguished, or dedicated he may be, can possibly know today what he will do in the stark conditions of nuclear warfare. Those circumstances which can be described are so obvious that they do not supply reassurance; the others simply multiply doubts. To try to discuss a common method for pushing the nuclear button—which is the most fateful decision that any political leader may have to make—before one has achieved a common foreign policy in East-West relations and in other matters seems to me to put the cart before the horse.

No magic formula will supply all the answers, but I can perhaps indicate the general direction in which I think we must move. We have to make up our minds that, no matter how serious may be our involvements in Vietnam and in other parts of the world, our international success or failure will ultimately be determined in the Atlantic area. If we cannot establish a cooperative relationship among nations representing such a pooling of power growing out of a common history and cultural background, and inheriting a similar political tradition, then we have very little chance of making an impact in other areas farther away from us both geographically and psychologically. Top priority, therefore, must continue to go to the Atlantic area. But we must recognize that the problem there has changed enormously during the past twenty years.

In the late 1940s the problem was one for which our national genius was particularly well suited: to restore the economies and to insure the military security of our allies. Today it is much more important for us to understand the nature of the historical evolution that we want to promote, and this is not so much a question of technical programs as it is a question of long-term political conceptions. As a nation that recently has been used to exercising an almost hegemonial relationship with its allies, we are pained to find our leadership challenged. The realization is all the more painful because most of those who still conduct our foreign policies were instrumental in creating the present pattern of relationships, and they find it hard to accept the fact that this pattern is under attack. Their natural impulse is to try to press matters back into as close an approximation to what is familiar as they can. I think in the long term this is disastrous.

In the long term, the question we have to answer is whether we want a Europe which does not have the physical ability to act autonomously, or whether it is wiser for us to concede Europe the physical capacity for autonomous action and to try to achieve common policies through common purpose. I believe that it is in our national interest, as well as in that of the Europeans, to encourage a much greater degree of European responsibility. I do not think that it is healthy for us, or for our allies, that we should be the country to make all the decisions, in every part of the globe, at every moment of time, over the indefinite future. There are those who say that this is beyond our physical resources; I am not certain that this is true, but I do fear that it is beyond our psychological resources. I do not think that our harassed decision-makers should fight for the privilege of taking on additional responsibility.

One reason why I have always been more sympathetic to De Gaulle than many of my colleagues and friends, and certainly most of the other contributors to this series, is not that I agree with his specific policies but that I respect his attempt to conduct an autonomous policy and, above all, to assert a responsible role for Europe. The great danger that I see is not in the challenge represented by De Gaulle but in a Europe that gives us no trouble, a Europe that turns inward, abdicating from international affairs. Such a Europe will in the long run be more dangerous to us than one that engages in a dialogue with us about the kind of world which we want to bring about. If we could bring ourselves to accept this conception, then many of the other problems would be more easily solved because we would then be able to distinguish irritants from long-term threats.

I feel also that a way to promote Atlantic unity under present circumstances is to declare a moratorium for a while on strategic questions, such as who presses the button in the inconceivable circumstance of general nuclear war, and instead to try to develop mechanisms by which common foreign policies can be conducted in the more frequent circumstances of day-to-day diplomacy, East-West relations, and disarmament negotiations. In 1958 it was proposed that a three-nation executive committee be established to coordinate the work of the Atlantic Alliance. That membership would be too limited, but it does seem to me that some kind of steering group for the Atlantic Alliance, one that is trying to look ahead over five or ten years to discern the kind of future to be built politically, and particularly that tries to develop common policies in East-West relations and on the issue of disarmament, would go a long way toward taking some of the sting out of the purely military debates which, in my judgment, are insoluble.

A few months ago I attended a conference of a number of leading private citizens of Europe and the United States. We were discussing, as always, who would order the use of nuclear weapons, when a Frenchman said something with which I heartily agree. He pointed out that it is absolutely futile to discuss plans for such an apocalyptic contingency. He then went on to say that the only way the Atlantic nations could come together is to find a way of dreaming together about the kind of world they want to bring about, rather than about the circumstances in which they might want to blow it up. We live in a world today which, because it is revolutionary, constantly confronts us with problems. Yet the crises of which we are most conscious are the ones least amenable to solutions, and the most obtrusive issues often are the least significant. It is impossible to create another world, or another structure, or another form of community, without a clear conception of a goal, but we deny ourselves such a conception by our intense preoccupation with the daily crises. This is really another way of saying that the reality that we could be building together depends, as my French friend observed, on the dreams that we should be dreaming together.

The Atlantic Community: Partners and Rivals

ANDRÉ PHILIP

DIFFICULTIES AND MISUNDERSTANDINGS ARE CURRENTLY DISRUPTING RELAtions between the United States and Europe, chiefly between the United States and France. If we wish to overcome these misunderstandings we must state our positions frankly and arrange a real confrontation of the differing points of view. Only after such an encounter will we be able to work out a democratic compromise between the conflicting opinions.

In discussing the Atlantic economy we shall focus on France's economic policy as it has evolved and as it is being expressed within the European Community today. We shall attempt to view this policy in the light of problems brought to our attention by the United States, on the one hand, and by the developing countries, on the other.

A useful point of departure is a discussion of France's present attitude, which is derived from the country's particular experiences since World War II. Prior to World War II France had been rather backward, both in agriculture and in industry. Since the Industrial Revolution began later, and proceeded at a slower pace in France than in other European countries, France did not experience the major periods of economic crisis and depression that other countries underwent in the nineteenth century. This stability, however, resulted in a slower rate of progress. After World War II France, entering both the agricultural and the industrial revolution, began to experience a tremendous change. The baby boom immediately after the war created more consumers for agriculture and industry, and the Underground Movement, in which everyone was risking his life every day, had produced a willingness to assume risks that had not been present before. France is in fact undergoing a complete technical revolution and is giving birth to a new social class of technicians, managers, inventors, and organizers.

This great change was not a product of the laissez-faire philosophy but of the French system of flexible, incentive planning. Immediately after the liberation France created a Department of Planning, which studies the possible patterns of evolution in the years to come and prepares the range of alternatives for the government. For example, the Department will present two, three, or four options: if the country is to obtain an increase of 6 per cent in the national income it must achieve a certain percentage increase in investments, in imports and exports, in individual consumption, and in other aspects of the economy; if the country is to secure only a 5 per-cent increase, it must attain proportionate increases in imports-exports, investments, and so forth. After the alternatives have been stated they are debated before the National Economic and Social Council, a body that contains delegates from all the major productive sectors of the country, for example, employers, workers, and farmers. This debate is followed by a debate in Parliament, and Parliament then chooses an increase of 4, 5, or 6 per cent. After taking action Parliament sends its decision back to the Department of Planning, which establishes modernization committees, corresponding to industrial sectors and the various regions of France. The modernization committees attempt to evaluate the plan for every industry and every region; the Department of Planning then reviews the results and elaborates the final plan, which is again presented to the National Economic and Social Council and ultimately to Parliament for final approval.

Each plan has two parts. The first is related to the public sector, the administration, and the nationalized industries. This part presents little difficulty, as the budget of the state is nothing more than the financial translation of the plan that has already been passed. In its second part, however, the plan pertains to the private sector, and acts only as an incentive, giving general directives. The credit and taxing policies, of course, do offer some interest and incitation to those who follow the plan and create some difficulties for those who go against its advice.

At present public opinion unanimously supports the general outline of the system. Initially the planners and the opponents of the plan engaged in ardent discussion. Even now discussion occurs between those who maintain that the plan relies too much on incitement and should be more compulsory and those who hold that it is too compulsory and should utilize more incentives, those who argue that the plan pertains only to economic life and should include a plan of incomes and those who are opposed to a plan of incomes. All this arguing, however, is within the system of planning; the system itself is accepted by everyone. It is a market system for both private and public enterprise, but it is a market system that operates under definite rules and by common cooperation to advance the aims of the plan. This background survey is necessary for a comprehensible discussion of other problems.

When the leaders of France chose flexible, contractual planning, they chose also to implement their choice within the larger European context. We were aware that it was impossible to have an economic and social policy for a country of only fifty million inhabitants when 250 million persons were the minimum needed to realize the contemporary industrial revolution. Today the growing belief is that even a community of 250 million is not sufficient. In the light of new technological progress the European Community of the Six is now the minimum. Great Britain should also be included, because the six countries of Europe alone are still too small to solve the problems of the most progressive industries. When France aligned itself with the European movement, however, the Six were the countries cooperating in it.

Two attitudes prevailed in Europe during the early stages of the movement. A number of persons sought to create a big European common market, and then to let competition work without any control. Others wanted to establish a European system of planning, somewhat along the lines the French had developed. They feared that if the market was enlarged to include Europe without expanding the methods of planning the French system of planning would be destroyed; the French, of course, wanted to preserve their system. Europeans entered into a hectic discussion of the two tendencies, and the Treaty of Rome, which created the European Community, represents a democratic compromise. From Article 2 of the Rome Treaty it is apparent that the aim of the signatory countries was to achieve among themselves a certain balanced growth of their economies through two instruments: the creation of a European customs union, and a growing coordination of their political, economic, and social policies. Thus one must be very cautious when speaking about these six countries. One should not refer to the "Community of the Six" as the "Common Market." It is the "European Community," an entity created by means of the Common Market and the coordination of policies.

To maintain a healthy balance between these two instruments for the realization of the European Community, another compromise—a quite new invention—was offered. As a means of ironing out differences between the federalists and the confederalists we invented the "commission system." A European Commission, whose members are appointed for a long period and are of independent standing, came into being. The Commission members work in conjunction with the Council of Ministers, who represent the interests of the various nation states, with a permanent dialogue between the two bodies. The Commission's task is to take the initiative in studying problems, formulate proposals, and then present these proposals to the Council of Ministers. The Council usually rejects the first proposal, and the Commission then submits another. After the fifth or sixth submission the Walls of Jericho come tumbling down and the proposal is accepted. Recently this procedure has been under dispute, but the Commission has finally had its essential power of initiative confirmed. This is a very important step.

Even though the compromise was an accepted procedure, a certain amount of difficulty had arisen in mid-1965 because the compromise was not kept in its entirety. We are ahead of schedule in the creation of the Common Market. Progress in this area has been rapid ever since the initial decision was taken to achieve a constant union through a series of steps in "x" number of years. In reality the process has evolved more quickly than expected. On January 1, 1966, a new 10 per cent reduction in intra-European tariffs brought the total reduction to 80 per cent. The remaining 20 per cent will be easy to eliminate, and everything is ready for the creation of a complete European customs union on January 1, 1967.

The coordination of economic and social policies, on the other hand, is behind schedule. Progress in this sphere is much more difficult, because the structure of each country's economic life is involved, and every change requires time. Some progress has been made in the standardization of railroad transportation, and a common method of establishing railroad tariffs is now practiced throughout the six countries. As the experience of the United States Interstate Commerce Commission exemplifies, this kind of agreement takes time and is rather difficult to achieve. Europe is making excellent progress also in the standardization of the indirect taxation system, and will introduce, probably in 1967, the added value tax in all six countries. The agreement to take this step has been made and needs only to be ratified by Parliament. This form of taxation has already been introduced progressively in seven other European countries.

One aspect in which no progress can be claimed is in the coordination of energy policies. At the beginning we believed that the creation of the European Coal and Steel Community was a step forward. That was when energy was coal; today energy is no longer coal but oil, natural gas, and increasingly atomic power. A conflict of interests on this question exists between the French and the Germans on one side, the other four on the other. The Germans (and the French) have large coal resources, and are therefore retreating slowly to avoid social difficulties with their miners. Countries like Belgium, Holland, and chiefly Italy, which are blessed with a lack of coal, purchase other sources of energy outside Europe in order to buy at cheaper prices. It is apparent that a number of factors must be considered, and that it will be very difficult to reach an agreement on European energy policy within the next few years, particularly in the light of uncertainties about what is going to occur in the field of atomic energy. We do know that 1970 will be a competitive year, but to what extent and in what proportion? Practically speaking, two or three years of study and discussion are necessary before a common energy policy can be elaborated.

The area in which we have had the most difficulty, as well as the greatest progress, has been in European agricultural policy. France is the largest agricultural producer in Europe, followed by Italy, and the French cost of production is the lowest of costs in the big European countries. Other countries, primarily Germany and Great Britain, produce agricultural products at a high cost and subsidize their farmers. At the same time, they import most of their food from areas outside Europe at a lower price than the French offer. They want to get a higher European price for their farm produce, while continuing to import from non-European areas at a low price. This, of course, does not at all suit the French, who want to have a lower European price at which everyone in Europe will buy.

You may be familiar with the settlement of the wheat problem. A European duty was placed on wheat imports from countries outside Europe, with the earnings from this duty to subsidize the exports of European wheat producers, essentially the French, to non-European areas. The wheat we export is the part of our crop we fail to sell in Europe because other Europeans purchase wheat outside Europe. Thus the importers will be subsidizing the exporters. That is the system agreed upon, but I think that it was a mistake. After a great deal of discussion among national interests, a compromise, essentially between French and German interests, was reached. The Commission in Brussels presented a proposal that was mathematically calculated to create the same amount of dissatisfaction in both France and Germany. The proposal was excellent from the psychological point of view, but it demonstrates that determining what a European agricultural policy should be is not an easy task.

It would have been better to decide whether to produce wheat first and export it outside Europe, or to produce meat—of which we are net importers—for which the demand is growing with the increasing incomes of the European people. A choice must be made: either wheat or meat. If it is wheat we can maintain our high price. If it is meat we must set a low wheat price and a high meat price. Unfortunately, the prices of wheat and meat were not fixed at the same time. There is an agreement on wheat, but none on meat. As a result, in the summer of 1965 the French farmers increased their wheat acreage. Now the French have so much wheat that they don't know what to do with it. Undoubtedly an outlet for it exists in underdeveloped countries suffering from hunger, and the French are going to give the wheat as a part of their aid to underdeveloped countries. But since the underdeveloped countries need meat and milk for the children, we should produce meat and milk in greater quantities. This is the point at which something is lacking in the European agricultural policy; it is the point over which a break occurred in June of 1965. Discussions are proceeding again, and we may hope that a common European agricultural policy on which there is complete agreement will emerge in the near future.

Along with progress toward European unification, and all the related difficulties, supplementary problems have come from other quarters: the "Kennedy Round" proposals; and the United Nations Conference on Trade and Development (UNCTAD), which was held in Geneva on the urging of the underdeveloped countries. President Kennedy proposed that all the big countries of the world negotiate a general tariff reduction of 50 per cent or more. At the same time strong pressure was placed on Great Britain to enter the European Community, and it was proposed that then all tariffs be abolished on those industrial products in which the enlarged Community and the United States conducted 80 per cent of "free world" trade. This would have created great difficulties in Europe for even the most progressive sectors.

Negotiations for Great Britain's entrance into the European Community began at that juncture. At the outset I was against these negotiations, because consideration of Britain's admission at a time when the Community had not yet been able to elaborate a common European agricultural policy would only have created more difficulties. The British wanted a situation similar to that requested by the Germans, but the British involved a much larger quantity. They wanted to enter the European Community, yet continue to buy all their food from non-European areas. If I were deeply in love with a beautiful girl who told me that after we were married she was going to eat all her meals away from home with another gentleman I would not marry her. I would remain in love with her, but before marrying her I would wait until she acquired the desire to be a housewife. Under such a condition Great Britain wanted to enter the Common Market. Today, under the British Labor Government, a much better basis on which Great Britain can enter the European Community is being established. Now Britain is not merely asking to enter the Market; it is also beginning to coordinate its economic policy with France's economic policy, and has made agreements with the various European nations on the aircraft industry, the space industry, and the electronic industry. This is the way to build up Europe; we must insist on this procedure, for the coordination of economic policies is much more important than the Market itself.

Now let us examine the present Kennedy Round negotiations, which are presenting a great problem to the European Community. The Rome Treaty states that the common European tariff, on the average, should be equal to the average of the six tariffs previously in existence. A tariff that is an average of the averages has been elaborated now, but it has not yet been put into effect. It will be put into operation when the European Community is in a state of complete customs union. How then can the Community negotiate a 50 per cent reduction in this tariff before such a tariff exists? Can a father and a mother in America sign a contract in the name of a yet unborn baby? This is precisely the situation we are negotiating—a reduction of one half of Europe's yet unborn tariff. If European economic integration had already been realized there would be no difficulty whatsoever. But, because the Community is behind schedule in economic integration, it has actually been building Europe around the tariff. Thus it would be dangerous to reduce the tariff if there is not at the same time definite and rapid progress toward economic integration. This is the position of the French government. France will negotiate the Kennedy Round reduction if definite progress toward the coordination of European economic policies is made simultaneously. A little progress toward European economic integration implies a small reduction in the Kennedy Round negotiations. Good progress toward European integration will facilitate a big reduction in the European tariff. In the Kennedy Round negotiations these two steps are linked.

Among other more important problems that Europe must also face, the first is the problem of research. America is now spending seven times more per capita on scientific industrial research than the countries of Europe are spending. American research is very well coordinated; it is curious that America, a country of so-called free enterprise, is the one country of the free world in which the state gives the highest percentage of public funds to finance research by private business. We believe that in the next ten years Europe must spend three times as much money on research as it does now, and that a European office must be established in Brussels to coordinate everything related to industrial research, primarily in the most progressive industries.

A second problem is that the first industry in Europe ranks thirty-seventh on an American list and that General Motors' business is larger than the national income of a country like Holland or Belgium. A great discrepancy exists, therefore, between European and American undertakings, and if we wish to be competitors we must begin to concentrate European industrial and financial resources. A proposal has been made to create a statute for European enterprise under a European legal statute. This statute would help prevent all the legal difficulties created by existing differences in the commercial laws of the six European countries.

If we push toward industrial and financial integration we risk the danger that the big European corporations could use their economic power against the interests of the consumers and could destroy the planning systems in some of our countries. This danger has already been treated in Articles 55 and 56 of the Rome Treaty; Article 55 is nothing new—similar provisions occur in the Sherman Act—but Article 56 does present new possibilities. It provides that the European Economic Commission can dissolve any European corporation that is guilty of abusive or excessive use of its economic power as defined in the theory of abusive power developed by the Conseil d'Etat in France. *Détournement de pouvoir et exces de pouvoir.* To determine an excessive abuse of power one must define the legitimate use of power, which, of course, is power used according to the plan. One must have a model by which to judge the activities of private enterprise. So on January 8, 1966, the European Economic Commission reported favorably on what they call a medium-period programmation. The Commission presented the report after a complete study by economists, technicians, and representatives of the governments of the six countries, and acceptance was unanimous, including German approval, which is absolutely essential. It is now possible that within the next few years we shall progress along the lines suggested in the report.

In addition to the difficulties of integration, a third problem facing the Community is that of American investments in Europe. On the whole, it is always good to have foreign investments in a country; foreign investments are investments, and investments create wealth. Foreign investors therefore have our approval, provided they invest when and where we want them to invest, that is, according to our plan. That is always the point to which we return. Periods of healthy economic development alternate with periods of inflation. In the latter situation it is better to put a brake on new investments, and we elaborate a policy of price stabilization to slow French investments during that period. It is essential to apply the same policy restrictions to foreign investments. In addition, France has a policy of regional development, and spends a great deal of money to induce French industries to move away from Paris and locate in Brittany or the southwest of France. If American investment likewise goes to Brittany and the southwest of France, hooray for American investment. If the Americans want to locate in Paris, however, the answer is no, because France is not spending money to move French industries in order to let American industries come in.

The principle denoted above applies to a number of sectors. Currently a very serious problem confronts the automobile industry. In recent years the industry has been growing twice as quickly as the average of French industrial production and twice as fast as the increase in the consumer's income. If it continues at that pace the gap between automobile production and the consumer's buying power will increase steadily. Until recently the gap has been filled successfully by exports; France is exporting more than one half of its automobile production. This obviously cannot continue; we shall have to establish a common policy for the merger of the automobile industry with specialized enterprises that are creating new lines of production to be developed if car manufacture declines. At present there is a great deal of discussion on this subject among European automobile industries. If the automobile industry does agree to work under a certain discipline and investment policy the agreement must not be destroyed by a dispute over General Motors' or Ford's freedom to invest anywhere without any discipline. They, too, must be a party to the agreement which is now being elaborated. Elaborating a common economic policy is the continuing problem.

A large French industry in computer production was another source of difficulty. General Electric bought the majority of shares in the company and began to close the research department, offering money to the French researchers to continue their work in America. Foreign capital is most welcome in France, as long as it does not obtain majority control and close the research department of an industry. We must have the rights of research, because it is the basis of our independence. The Six European countries are now studying this problem in an attempt to work out the details of a common statute for extra-European investments; the statute will give guarantees and will stipulate certain conditions, including degree of European control.

Europe also has a monetary problem. We are now on the gold standard of exchange, and under this system two foreign currencies—the pound and the dollar—are accepted as reserve currency throughout the world. It is obvious that our British friends cannot continue to carry this burden. They have financial difficulties stemming primarily from the fact that they are too small a country to have their currency used as reserves for the entire Commonwealth. One of the reasons behind their interest in entering the European Community is a desire to have the Community share with them the financing of the British Commonwealth. The United States has its problem because it can create currency which is accepted as reserve all over the world and thus can be used to finance American investments abroad. The French government rather objects to this system, and President de Gaulle made in 1965 a statement that I think was entirely out of line. He suggested replacing the present gold standard with the old gold standard. In reality it is impossible to revert to the old gold standard because it never really existed. What was called the gold standard in the nineteenth century was a sterling standard, financed entirely through the city of London. Now it is impossible to return to any gold standard because the supply of gold is insufficient to finance all of the world's trade. Nor would it be wise to try to increase the price of gold. I do not have enough sympathy for either of the world's two biggest producers of gold—South Africa and Russia—to give them such a tremendous gift. Instead of a return to a gold standard, the creation of a world supplementary unit should be attempted—a solution similar to the clearing-union proposal made by Lord Keynes at the Bretton Woods Conference immediately after the war. In addition to gold, there would be a monetary unit, issued by a world bank according to needs imposed by the evolution of world trade and according to the average prices of world trade, which the bank would seek to keep as stable as possible.

Problems other than those relating to the United States arose in 1965 at the United Nations Conference on Trade and Development in Geneva, at which I led the French delegation. We speak in general terms of helping the underdeveloped countries, but at the time of the Conference we had done very little to help them. The Gospel says that the right hand must not know what the left hand is doing, but while our Christian left hand was giving help to the underdeveloped countries, our free-enterprise right hand was taking more from their pockets than they received. These emerging countries have lost more in the last ten years through reductions in the price of tropical raw materials which they were selling than they have received in aid from the industrialized countries. The first task is not to encourage them to produce and export more of what they are now producing and exporting in quantity, but to stabilize prices by organizing the markets for these products. At the same time, they must be encouraged to create new lines of production so that they can diversify their exports and be freed from their present dependence on one or two products.

At the Geneva Conference those who advocated a tariff reduction and a policy of laissez faire to help these poor countries clashed with those who wanted to organize the market and pursue a policy of stabilizing world prices. They discussed at length the infant industries of the developing countries. Some industrialized countries, for example the United States, said, "Just wait until after the results of the Kennedy

Round; the tariffs will then be so greatly reduced that they will be able to sell in Europe or in America." I cannot see how a new infant industry, which is not yet competitive, could possibly sell in Europe in competition with American exporters, or in America in competition with European exporters. In both cases it would be thrown out of the market. It is more in the interest of infant industries to have the already industrialized countries proceed slowly in the Kennedy Round and maintain a 10- to 15-per-cent tariff. The suppression of this tariff in Europe for underdeveloped countries, but not for the United States, and in the United States for underdeveloped countries, but not for Europe, would give a 10- to 15-per-cent competitive advantage to the underdeveloped countries in relation to other competitors. In place of the traditional most-favored-nation clause, we therefore propose preferential agreements negotiated with regional groups of the developing countries.

And then comes the problem of aid. In the nineteenth century, private capital from England went into the United States and the Commonwealth territories, which at that time were the underdeveloped countries. Why can't private capital do so now? It is a fact that American capital is currently being invested in Europe because it earns larger returns there than in the underdeveloped countries. Perhaps people are also less enthusiastic about putting their money into the underdeveloped countries now, because most of the capital that was invested there in the nineteenth century was lost. The capital that does go into the underdeveloped countries is invested in very specialized kinds of production—such as plantations and mining—and is not always in the best long-term interest of the country concerned. I know of an African country that has wonderful waterfalls and bauxite deposits. Private capital is interested in harnessing the waterfall to produce high-powered electricity, and in exploring the bauxite deposits in the hope of building an aluminum plant. When companies operate in this manner they call on ten thousand native workers to come from their villages, thus destroying the whole structure of the African village. Afterwards, when the dam and the plant are built, they don't need all the manpower, and the workers are dismissed—with nowhere to go. If investors choose to proceed in this fashion they must at the same time be compelled to finance a policy of agricultural development, so that despite the departure of a number of men the village can continue to produce. They must also prepare for the creation of small consumer industries to provide work for the natives when they are no longer building dams and plants. Private capital is valuable if it is used within the general planning system of the country and in combination with policies for agricultural development and for the development of consumer industries. If investments are not so coordinated economic and social disaster results within the country concerned. Private capital is useful, but since there is not enough of it we must try to elaborate together a world policy for underdeveloped countries.

At Geneva I moved that the UNCTAD adopt a resolution asking all advanced industrial nations to recognize their duty to devote 1 per cent of their national income to help underdeveloped countries. This resolution was passed unanimously; only the Russians abstained with this reservation: "All the capitalist countries must make this contribution to the poor, underdeveloped countries that they used to exploit. But as we are not a capitalist country and have never conquered anyone nor dominated anyone, we don't owe anyone anything. With our good heart we will do a great deal, but we refuse to be under legal or ethical obligations to do anything." The developing countries, needless to say, resented this typically paternalistic manner of presentation. But the commitment of 1 per cent is significant. A commitment to give one per cent of our national income to help underdeveloped countries means that we cannot make a choice. We cannot say that we will give it to our friends and refuse our enemies. It means that we will give it to anyone who is making an effort at economic development in any legal or political system. This is the attitude that the French government takes. It doesn't care about the political situation in developing countries. It will give continuing technical and financial help regardless of the changes that may occur in government. Changes in government occur often and quickly in many of these countries, and the readjustment of our aid policy each time would create a great deal of trouble. It is much wiser to guarantee that we will continue the aid regardless of what happens, and carry on by negotiating with the regional groups in the different systems of planning.

In Geneva two differing outlooks prevailed. One group advocated laissez faire. Now what does that term really mean? If we suppressed all the tariffs in the world on bananas, would the small producers of bananas get their fair share of trade in a market dominated by United Fruit? I don't know precisely what the international market price is for coffee or for cocoa, but I do know that when I drink a cup of coffee or cocoa in my country, France, only 10 per cent of the price I pay goes to the African producer. When the product is loaded aboard a ship in an African harbor its value is 35 per cent of that price; when it is unloaded on to the docks of Marseilles it is 45 per cent. More than one half of the price that I finally pay remains in my own country in consumer's tax, in freight, and in profits for the import-export companies. Shall world trade be controlled by the import-export companies, or by big interterritorial corporations like the oil corporations, which will entirely dominate the market? France is trying a third alternative. It made an agreement with the Algerian government to create a cooperative association for all production, refining, and transportation. If the world has private companies why shouldn't it have public companies, and mixed-economy companies, created by intergovernmental agreements? If these agreements are made both the producer and the consumer will have the right and the opportunity to follow a product until it reaches the consumer, instead of letting tradesmen control the middle steps and thereby dominate both producer and consumer.

I have tried to present a range of economic problems facing Europe today. We don't agree with present United States policy, but I think that policy will change. It is changing within the United States; so it may also change within the realm of international negotiations. Europe and the United States see problems from different perspectives; so everyone needs to explain his position. The differing points of view must be the subjects of international discussions and confrontations without taboos. Everything should be discussed—free enterprise, laissez faire, the old free-trade method. Let us discuss, let us juxtapose the various policies, and when all the arguments have been presented and everything has been clearly analyzed, let us work out a compromise: a common world policy on aid to underdeveloped countries and a common trade policy among industrialized nations.

Germany, the Continuing Challenge

HANS SPEIER

AT THE END OF WORLD WAR II ALL CAPITALS OF CENTRAL AND EASTERN EUROPE and their surrounding areas lay in the Soviet sphere of influence: Warsaw, Berlin, Prague, Vienna, Budapest, Belgrade, Bucharest, and Sofia. For a while, the Kremlin tried to extend its influence even farther to the west. The Russians not only demanded large reparations from those parts of Germany that were occupied by the Western allies, but also attempted to participate in allied control over the heavy industry of the Ruhr, and they violated the agreements reached at the wartime conferences. The hopes and expectations of many Americans in high office vanished: the wartime alliance disintegrated because of the new danger that all of Europe might come under Russian control. This danger had to be averted by the United States, since neither Britain nor France nor any combination of West European powers could avert it. The measures for the economic recovery of Western Europe and for its effective military defense required that West Germany be permitted to participate in this process under special safeguards tying her securely to the Western powers. Europe and Germany were divided and have remained so ever since.

The dividing line between the Communist states and the non-Communist countries that runs through Central Europe splits Germany into two parts. Indeed, since 1961 her former capital, situated more than a hundred miles behind the Iron Curtain, is itself partitioned by a wall that separates more than a million people living under Communist rule in the Eastern sector of the city from more than two million West Berliners living prosperously in freedom, though in the midst of Communist Germany.

Two other parts of the former Reich, lying farther to the east, were lost in consequence of World War II to the Soviet Union and Poland. The first part comprises a slice of former East Prussia with the city of Königsberg, now Kaliningrad, where the German philosopher Immanuel Kant was born. When this part of Germany was annexed by the Soviet Union in 1945 only a few thousand Germans were still living there. The others had been killed or had fled westward.

The other, larger, eastern part of the Reich became Polish. It comprises the southern slice of former East Prussia, Silesia, and the Eastern section of Pomerania and Brandenburg. These so-called Oder-Neisse territories were given to Poland in compensation for Eastern Poland, which was also annexed by the Soviet Union. Prior to World War II about ten million Germans had lived in these territories. Of these about 1.5 million persons perished either while fleeing or while being deported. Most of the remaining eight million Germans were forced to migrate to West Germany, while Polish refugees from Eastern Poland and Poles from Central Poland were resettled in turn in the vacated new western provinces of Poland. In 1965 approximately one quarter of all Poles (about 8.5 million) lived in the Oder-Neisse territories. It has been estimated that of these about one half were born or brought up there.[1]

West Germany is a member of the Western European Union, which includes Great Britain but not the United States; of NATO, which will soon exist without France; of the Common Market, which includes France but not Great Britain; and of various other Western international organizations. The West German economy has close ties through trade and investment with Western Europe and the United States. In contrast, Communist Germany belongs to Communist international organizations, such as the Warsaw Pact, the counterpart of NATO in the East, and COMECOM, which serves the economic integration of Eastern Europe with the Soviet Union. The Communist German Democratic Republic is also tied bilaterally to the Soviet Union by a special friendship pact. Compared with this pact, West Germany's bilateral friendship treaty with France is of less importance, because it was ratified by the West German Parliament with a Preamble stipulating that the treaty be subordinated to the Atlantic ties of the Federal Republic. Until now the friendship treaty has failed to serve French ambitions to pry West Germany loose from the United States. In 1964 and 1965 German officials adopted the habit of saying that Bonn could never choose between Washington and Paris, since it needed both Atlantic and Continental ties for its security and well being. In fact, on no political, military, or economic issue of consequence has Bonn ever dared to please Paris when this might have offended Washington. Indeed, it would not have been in Bonn's interest to make such a choice.

II

The integration of the two parts of Germany into the Western and Eastern political orbits, respectively, has darkened the prospect of German reunification by peaceful means, and fortunately no government thinks of reunification by other means. Communist ideas on the German problem differ so radically from Western policies that it is realistic to expect that the present unsettled state of affairs will not change for some time to come.

The Communists point to the *facts* in Europe and urge their formal international

[1] Georg Bluhm, *Die Oder-Neisse-Linie in der deutschen Aussenpolitik* (Freiburg: Verlag Rombach, 1963).

recognition; the Western powers insist with decreasing urgency on their *right* to change the facts by international negotiation. The Communists still insist that the Western powers, including West Germany, ought to recognize the Communist East German regime. Such recognition would mean acceptance of the Communist doctrine that there are in fact two legitimate German governments and two German states. To these might have to be added a third independent German state, that of the so-called "Free City" of West Berlin, in which the military presence of the Western powers would have to be abolished or to be augmented by Soviet contingents, or to be replaced by a United Nations force.[2]

The Communist view of a desirable order in Europe includes the recognition by all Western powers of the frontier between East Germany and Poland, the so-called Oder-Neisse Line, which, according to the Potsdam Agreement of 1945, remains to be definitely drawn when the German peace treaty will be agreed upon. At present this border is recognized by East Germany but not by the Federal Republic—a fact which has strained the relations between Poland and West Germany. Or, to put it differently, it has increased the leverage that the Soviet Union has on Polish foreign policy, since the Poles fear German demands of territorial restitution at Poland's expense.

In West Germany no political party at this time dares to suggest the recognition of the Oder-Neisse frontier for fear that the rival parties would benefit from loud patriotic protests to such a concession. The Federal Republic claims to be the only legitimate German government, and the governments of the other Western powers support this claim. At best, only a coalition government, composed of all West German political parties, could afford to recognize Poland's western frontier. But even then such an act might well bring to the fore immediately or at a later date, for example, at the time of an economic depression, dormant nationalist forces that would organize themselves against the existing political parties on an antidemocratic basis. Nationalist feelings, instead of being captured by an existing party, might be the ferment in the formation of a new party turning against the West German Establishment, as it were. Perhaps it is even more important to consider that the recognition of the Oder-Neisse Line would not necessarily lead to an easing of international tensions between West Germany and her Eastern neighbors. Nothing could prevent Communists in Poland, East Germany, and the Soviet Union from doubting the good faith of the West German government, were it to recognize the frontier. Thus the Communists might celebrate the collapse of the sound legal position of the West by adding insult to a self-inflicted injury on the Western cause.

---

[2] Cf. Alois Riskin, *Das Berlinproblem* (Cologne: 1964); see also Hans Speier, *Divided Berlin* (New York: Prager, 1961).

The crux of the problem of German reunification is not the border problem, but the question of military security. The West Germans feel the threatening presence of more than twenty Soviet divisions in East Germany and eight hundred or more Soviet medium-range missiles that are pointed at them. They are also disturbed by the ominous language of the Soviet leaders who have not hesitated to compare West Germany's fate in another world war with that of "a veritable graveyard"[3] or with "a candle . . . that would burn up . . . in the first hour."[4] Russia and her European allies fear, or claim to fear, the military might of NATO to which the Federal Republic contributes the strongest conventional force—twelve divisions—in Central Europe. They also fear that West Germany will get access to nuclear weapons.

The western powers have not taken any initiative for the last eight years to renew negotiations with the Soviet Union on the reunification of Germany. Even in West Germany, where official spokesmen persistently point out that reunification remains a basic aim of West German foreign policy and where according to public opinion polls the interest in reunification is increasing, it is generally accepted today that the day of reunification lies somewhere in the distant future.

In the meantime the United States continues to voice its support of the German official position on reunification. So do the other NATO powers at more or less regular intervals—at the NATO Council meetings and on other solemn occasions. The United States has made it clear, however, that it expects the Germans to reconsider the problem in all its implications, including the problem of security and the border issue, and to come up with suggestions of their own as to what ought to be done. Agreement would have to be reached among the Western Allies before the Soviet leaders are approached once more.

Furthermore, the U. S. government has repeatedly emphasized that reunification may eventually be attained by an "indirect approach," that is, by a loosening of the ties that bind the East European states to the Soviet Union. Much has been said in this context about East-West trade, cultural exchange, and other cooperative measures. It is hoped that this policy of "bridge building" will create a political climate in which Eastern and Western Europe will once again see their common interest in cooperation with one another. Both President Kennedy and President Johnson, as well as General de Gaulle, have intimated that in their views the reunification of Germany may have to await the time when Europe as a whole is less sharply divided than it is today.

This policy seems reasonable enough, as long as the Germans are willing to abide by its long-range terms and put up with American passivity. The Federal Republic

[3] Soviet note to the Federal Republic, April 27, 1957.
[4] Khrushchev's statement in East Berlin, January 16, 1963.

has been willing to do so, as was made evident once more by the diplomatic note of March 25, 1966, sent to all governments with which it maintains diplomatic relations and also to Eastern European and Arab countries with which it does not.[5] The notes, described by German officials as a peace offensive, proposed a series of nonaggression pacts with the Soviet Union, Poland, Czechoslovakia, and any other European state that might desire such a pact. In addition, Bonn declared that it would be willing to conclude bilateral agreements with the Soviet Union and East European countries on the exchange of military observers to attend maneuvers of each other's armed forces. Finally, in an effort to answer "the monotonous propaganda" concerning German "aggressiveness," Bonn proposed various measures in the field of arms control and disarmament.

At the same time Bonn said in its note that "all efforts to achieve security, disarmament, and armaments control will fail to bring decisive and lasting success" unless the causes of tensions are simultaneously removed step by step; in Europe this would mean "above all . . . granting to the entire German nation the right freely to determine its political way of life and its destiny."[6] As regards the border issue, the Federal Republic reiterated its well-known position: "Under the allied agreements of 1945 the settlement of frontier questions has been postponed until the conclusion of a peace treaty with the whole of Germany and that according to international law Germany continues to exist within its frontiers of December 31, 1937, until such time as a freely elected all-German government recognizes other frontiers."[7] The only new tone on the frontier issue could be detected in the following passage of the German note: "If, when the occasion arises, the Poles and the Germans enter into negotiations on frontier questions in the same spirit that led to the conciliation between Germany and her Western neighbors, then Poles and Germans will also find their way to agreement. For in this question neither emotions nor alone the power of the victor, but rather reason, must prevail."[8]

Despite this note and many other solemn declarations by German officials, the Federal Republic has shown as little real initiative on reunification as have the other Western powers; nor can it be taken for granted that in the prevailing circumstances the cause of reunification would be served if Bonn were to abandon its present position. In addition to the argument advanced before, it may be noted that official indications of West German willingness to recognize the Oder-Neisse Line prior to the conclusion of a peace treaty might encourage Germany's allies to narrow the gap be-

---

[5] For the English translation of this note see *The Bulletin*, issued by the Press and Information Office of the German Federal Government, Bonn, March 29, 1966. The only countries to which the note was not sent were the German Democratic Republic, Communist China, Nationalist China, North Korea, North Vietnam, and Albania.

[6] *Ibid.*   [7] *Ibid.*   [8] *Ibid.*

tween their declaratory policy on reunification and their operative policy on the status quo in Europe. Indeed, some Germans believe that action by the Federal Republic on the frontier issue at this time would make it easier for the United States and the Soviet Union to extend their *détente* instead of shortening the waiting time to the day of reunification.

While at present the West Germans seem willing to live without hope that German reunification will be attained in the foreseeable future, it would be folly to disregard the possibility that German disappointment and impatience may grow. The key to reunification lies in Moscow, and Moscow cannot be assumed to have completely discounted the possibility of the Federal Republic's sometime becoming more receptive than it has been in the past to Soviet overtures on Soviet-German conciliation at the expense of other NATO powers. Such a major political move by the Kremlin remains a Soviet option. The important safeguards against its successful exercise are, of course, Bonn's close ties with the West.

In recent months, while everything has appeared as calm and unchanged as ever on the surface of Bonn's policy on reunification, various factors have indicated that pressure for breaking the long-lasting impasse may come from Germans *outside* the government—the churches, other social organizations, and the intellectuals. Thus, in 1965, a Memorandum of the Evangelical Church, advocating a moral and political reëxamination and, possibly, a revision of official policy regarding the territories lost to Poland, caused a passionate public discussion throughout West Germany.[9] Furthermore, several well-known Germans have found a wide echo for their proposals of more energetic and imaginative German policies on reunification.[10] A so-called "scenario" of the future course of events in Europe, that is, a fictional account by Rüdiger Altmann of the gradual achievement of German reunification on November 1, 1976, has been presented and subsequently discussed on German television in violation of many time-honored tabus regarding cooperation between West and East Germany.[11] Again, an unorthodox "catechism" on the German problem, fiercely attacking the legal and political foundations of Adenauer's and Erhard's policy has aroused the attention of German intellectuals.[12] It is a common mistake of those who

---

[9] Cf. *Die Lage der Vertriebenen und das Verhältnis des deutschen Volkes zu seinen östlichen Nachbarn* (Hanover: Verlag des Amtsblatts der Evangelischen Kirche in Deutschland, 1965, 44 pp.).

[10] Cf. especially, Wilhelm Wolfgang Schütz, *Reform der Deutschland Politik* (Cologne and Berlin: Kiepenheuer und Witsch, 1965).

[11] *Stern*, a widely read illustrated weekly, published the discussion of the scenario in its issue of April 17, 1966.

[12] "Katechismus zur deutschen Frage," *Kursbuch*, ed. Hans Magnus Enzensberger, No. 4, 1966, pp. 1–55.

read political literature to overestimate the influence of intellectuals in Germany because modern intellectuals quickly publish what they think. Nonetheless, it has become a fairly common practice in Germany to heap scorn on Bonn's alleged lack of realism and to speak in public about West German cooperation with East German Communists as something that is inevitable or humane or clever or simply desirable. Prior to the erection of the Berlin Wall in August 1961, and the first agreement on the Berlin border passes of December 1963, such talk was less frequently heard.

All these ventures of German intellectuals on the television screen, on the stage of political cabarets, in periodicals and paperbacks, and occasionally in discussion of restless student groups have one thing in common: a kind of German "nationalism" which, if anything, is "neutralist" rather than anti-Communist. The intellectuals who promote this neutralism are inspired neither by militarist nor National Socialist nor Prussian leanings.[13] Instead, they are more or less critical of American as well as French policies, although their main criticism, which used to be focused on Dr. Adenauer as long as he was Chancellor, is now centered on the government headed by Chancellor Erhard;[14] Professor Erhard, the hope of German intellectuals as long as Adenauer wielded power, has become an object of their condescension.

Far more important than the behavior of the German intellectuals is the recent exchange of letters between the East German Socialist Unity Party (Sozialistische Einheitspartei Deutschlands, SED) and the Social Democratic Party (Sozialdemokratische Partei, SPD) on the arrangement of public debates between prominent East German Communists and West German Socialist leaders in East and West Germany. The initiative was taken in February, 1966, by Walter Ulbricht's Communists. Willy Brandt's Socialists, while rejecting any kind of "popular-front policy," accepted the challenge. In their second letter they named Willy Brandt, Herbert Wehner, and Fritz Erler as their representatives in the debates.[15]

---

[13] The book by Hans-Georg von Studnitz, *Bismarck in Bonn* (Stuttgart: Seewald Verlag, 1964) is an exception, but it has had no visible impact on the intellectual climate in West Germany, whereas Peter Bender's *Offensive Entspannung* (Cologne and Berlin: Kiepenheuer und Witsch, 1964), which strongly advocated increased contacts with communist East Germany, became a best-seller and was republished in installments by the most widely read German weekly, *Der Spiegel*.

[14] To complicate the issue further, Dr. Adenauer, always the *bête noire* of liberal German intellectuals because of his anti-Communist "Cold War policy," declared on March 21, 1966, that the Soviet Union "had entered the circle of nations that want peace." It was Erhard who said the next day that until "the test case" for Soviet "peacefulness" had been dealt with in Europe it was important "not to indulge in fantasies, and not to chase after illusions" (*Die Welt*, March 23, 1966).

[15] At the time this is being written four letters have been exchanged and published in many German newspapers, namely (1) an "Open Letter," dated February 7, 1966, ad-

The Social Democrats regarded the publication of their first reply to Ulbricht in *Neues Deutschland,* the chief newspaper in East Germany, as an important success, since this letter contained some sharp criticism of Ulbricht's policy. Their feelings of triumph may be compared with the satisfaction felt by the Kennedy Administration when the President's interview with Khrushchev's son-in-law was published in Moscow in December 1961. The real significance of the exchange of letters between SED and SPD, however, seems to lie elsewhere.

First, Willy Brandt regards the public correspondence and the arrangements for public debates between Communist and Social Democratic leaders as efforts "to maintain contact between the divided parts of the population." Brandt's perspicacity on these efforts is beyond question; he sees them in the perspective of previous contacts made in divided Germany by means of interzonal trade, the bridge over the River Saale, built by East Germans with West German funds, the creation of an all-German Olympic team, and the various "pass agreements" enabling West Berliners to visit relatives in East Berlin for a limited time.[16] Indeed, the new developments may be understood as an outgrowth of the policy of "the little steps" to bring East and West Berlin together *despite the Wall*; this policy was launched with the first border-pass agreement of December 1963. Ulbricht's new initiative would hardly have been successful had it not been for the preceding agreements to which Brandt correctly called attention.

Secondly, the exchange of letters and the arrangements that may result from it replace governmental policy on reunification by action of political parties (and possibly other social organizations, such as trade unions). It also substitutes talk for action: while Communists and Social Democrats debate in Chemnitz or Hanover, the East German police can continue to shoot at Germans wanting to escape across the

---

dressed "to the delegates of the Party Conference of the SPD in Dortmund and to friends of Socialdemocracy in West Germany"; it was signed by Walter Ulbricht, First Secretary, for the Central Committee of the Socialist Unity Party of Germany; (2) "Open Reply of the SPD to the 'Open Letter' of the SED of February 7," dated March 18, 1966; (3) a second "Open Letter" by the SED, dated March 25, and (4) a second "Open Reply" by the SPD, published in several West German newspapers on April 16. For the texts of (1) and (2) cf. *Europa Archiv,* Bonn, Vol. 7, April 10, 1966, pp. D177–D188; for the texts of (3) and (4) cf. *Frankfurter Allgemeine Zeitung,* April 16, 1966. For a review of previous Communist attempts to establish contacts with West German politicians, which date back to 1950, cf. the articles by Dettmar Cramer in *Frankfurter Allgemeine Zeitung,* April 5, 1966, and the excerpts from a series of interviews conducted by Hans Ulrich Kempski in 1958 with Walter Ulbricht, Ernst Lemmer, and Herbert Wehner in *Süddeutsche Zeitung,* April 16–17, 1966.

[16] Cf. Willy Brandt's interview in *Der Spiegel,* March 28, 1966.

Wall. The order to shoot need not be rescinded; indeed, Ulbricht coldly stated in his second letter that he had no intention of doing so.

Third, despite Brandt's strange disparagement of inquiries into the motives of Ulbricht's initiative[17] it is fairly obvious what they are. The SED wants to weaken the support of Bonn's policy on reunification by the Social Democrats, create strife among and within the West German parties, and, above all, mobilize West German acceptance of two legitimate German states. Ulbricht is flexible in his tactics but adamant in the pursuit of his political aims. He has characterized the policy of the Federal Republic on reunification as an evident failure and invited the SPD to talk about political subjects: negotiations between the two German governments, preparation of a peace treaty, disarmament and European security, etc. By contrast the SPD has declared that its representatives would speak "in both states [*sic!*] about the key problem of German politics, which today seems, above all, how the life of the human beings in divided Germany can be made easier."[18] This laudably humanitarian emphasis, which occurs repeatedly in the SPD letters, misses the thrust of Ulbricht's political initiative. Undoubtedly, "millions of human beings" are "vividly interested," as the SPD claims, in "neighborly traffic at the zonal border according to the model of the Berlin pass agreements; in further steps in the direction of [*sic!*] free movement of persons in Berlin itself; in possibilities of the sale and, respectively, postal delivery of newspapers and periodicals in both parts of Germany; in the dismantling of unnecessary shackles on exchanges in the fields of economy, science, and culture."[19] But what is the political weight of these "key problems?" What is their relation to Ulbricht's questions on war and peace, European security, and "democracy," as he understands it? Is Ulbricht right when he claims in his second letter that "the postwar period has come to an end?" In the letter by the SPD the reference to "the two German states" is especially unfortunate. It was made at about the same time that the three Western powers were resisting East Germany's effort to become a member of the United Nations. In a letter to the president of the Security Council, dated March 16, 1966, the United States, the United Kingdom, and France again rejected "attempts to establish the so-called German Democratic Republic as an independent state."[20]

---

[17] "I should like to renounce the philosophizing about the motives of others [*sic*]. It is no substitute for political action which immediately makes it clear who wants what and whether there are perhaps small chances for a development in the interest of human beings." Cf. Willy Brandt interview in *Der Spiegel*, March 28, 1966.

[18] Second SPD letter; see n. 15.

[19] *Ibid*.

[20] German text in *Europa Archiv*, Vol. 7, April 10, 1966, p. D196. The SPD emphasis on the welfare of the "human beings" on "the other side" (a favorite new euphemism for

Although Ulbricht's latest political move has already succeeded in driving a wedge between the Christian Democrats and the Social Democrats,[21] it is too early to predict its ultimate results. Many Socialists hope to promote beneficent changes in East German policy and leadership by their response. Other observers fail to share this optimism, and notice instead the ease with which the second strongest party in West Germany has reconciled its anti-Communism with calculations stemming from humanitarianism, latent disappointment about the passivity of the Western powers on the German problem, and frustrated domestic political ambitions.

The first two rounds of correspondence have indeed shown that tendencies toward a quasi-political or unpolitical neutralism are no longer confined to intellectuals in Germany. Should such neutralism spread and entail some benefits—humanitarian or otherwise—the spectrum of future German challenges to American foreign policy will be significantly enlarged. The Federal Republic may either move in the direction of greater indifference toward the territorial status quo in Europe, accepting the emergence of a new nationalist opposition as a tolerable risk, or it may become more responsive to Soviet blandishments in the hope of furthering its professed national aims. It is not even entirely impossible that new West German leaders may yet seek solace from disappointment with American policy by playing second fiddle in a European concert composed by De Gaulle. Of these three possibilities, the first probably is the course that events are most likely to take, if German neutralism should indeed gain respectability.

[EDITOR'S NOTE. The debates did not take place. With the first one scheduled for July 14, 1966, and a "safe-conduct law" enacted by the West German Parliament to permit Communists to speak in West Germany without fear of arrest, the East German government called off the project in early July. That government professed of-

---

the Communist party of Germany) has its precedent in the language of SED functionaries at a time when they regarded their regime as weak in 1950. In December of that year Herr Diedermann, president of the East German *Volkskammer* wrote to Herr Ehlers, president of the West German *Bundestag*, about the "West German brothers and sisters" in our "common fatherland" and declared, "lest this artificial alienation lead to Germany's being definitely torn asunder and then to the decline of the German nation, we must scale the artificial barriers that have been erected in all these years and get together as German human beings" (quoted by Dettman Cramer, in *Frankfurter Allgemeine Zeitung*, April 6, 1966).

[21] A Christian Democrat deputy warned against "a euphoria of all-German conversations" (*Die Welt,* April 6, 1966); Erhard himself expressed disapproval of "a personality occupying an official position" (i.e., Brandt) debating in East Germany (*Die Welt,* April 16); and a spokesman for the Free Democratic Party criticized the remarks of a government spokesman who had failed to endorse the SPD action (*ibid.*).

fense at the existence of such a law, or the need for it, and called for its repeal and for SPD disavowal of the Federal Republic's policies vis-à-vis East Germany, as preliminaries to a renewal of discussions about the debates. Many Western observers judged that the East German government, perhaps under Soviet pressure, had decided that it would be politically unwise or even dangerous to permit the debates to proceed at this time, and thus had sought a way out. Brandt and the SPD leadership rejected the East German conditions, but continued the search for channels of political conversation. One suggestion was that East German leaders might be invited to speak in a televised panel discussion on West German TV.]

III

Ever since the resolution of the Cuban missile crisis in October 1962, the overt Communist threats to Western Europe have abated. At present American policy in Europe is hampered primarily by Paris rather than Moscow. The Soviet leaders can view with satisfaction the fact that the cohesion of the North Atlantic Alliance is jeopardized by internal strife. In this situation they can bide their time and adopt a waiting strategy punctuated only by vehement attacks on the alleged aggressiveness of the Federal Republic of Germany and by applause for De Gaulle.

It is by no means certain, however, that the Soviet government will forever confine its hostility to the West to propaganda, to obstructionism on arms control and disarmament measures, and to the support of what Khrushchev chose to call "wars of liberation" in Asia and Africa. The sense of relief induced by President Kennedy's success in averting a major war at the time of the Cuban missile crisis must not be permitted to obscure the fact that it was Khrushchev, the promoter of coexistence, who put the missiles on Cuban soil in the first place. It would be folly to assume that serious conflict between the United States and the Soviet Union in Europe or elsewhere will never recur, merely because Khrushchev once agreed to remove offensive Soviet weapons from Cuba. Nor are there any good reasons for assuming that another confrontation between the United States and the Soviet Union would be treated by both sides with the same restraint and caution as was the Cuban missile crisis and that there would be as much time to settle it as there was in October 1962. Unfortunately, we have no way of knowing whether in this regard the historic crisis of 1962 was a historical precedent or an historical exception. In any event, neither the Sino-Soviet split nor internal changes in the Communist orbit of Europe, neither the Soviet withdrawal in 1962 nor various agreements on relatively minor issues that the United States and the Soviet Union have reached since that time, neither American strategic superiority over Russia nor the ability of each nuclear giant to destroy the other—none of these facts warrant the conclusion that the probability of serious political conflict and of limited or general war between the two world powers has been permanently reduced. American and NATO political and military planning must continue to concern itself with such contingencies. One of the major contingencies would be the renewal of sharp conflict in Europe, directly or indirectly affecting the status of Germany.

The Soviet Union still is the most powerful adversary of the United States.[22] Red China's gross national product today is about one fourth that of the Soviet Union. The military outlays of these two Communist powers are, roughly speaking, in the ratio of one to eight. The Soviet Union, and not Red China, has a large nuclear arsenal at the present time. France and China are at least ten years behind the nuclear development of each of the two giant powers, and neither the Soviet Union nor the United States is likely to stand still for ten years while China and France make costly efforts to advance their nuclear technology and production. One sample situation will illustrate: we have heard a great deal from French spokesmen about the strategic importance of the French nuclear force. It is now common knowledge that the American withdrawal of the nuclear weapons that were assigned to the small French forces stationed in West Germany will deprive France of many times the number of nuclear warheads she has produced herself. This example contains a lesson that applies to China as well. Talk about the so-called "nuclear club" and the dangers of nuclear proliferation should not blur our understanding that there are nuclear giants and nuclear dwarfs, and that it is extremely difficult for the nuclear dwarfs to become giants or to hold their own against them. Foreign policy is concerned with the current situation, and its time horizon cannot easily extend beyond five to ten years. Within this horizon the Soviet Union and not Red China remains the main adversary of the United States.

Europe is still the focus of American foreign policy, because it is of vital interest to the United States not to permit the old continent to fall under the domination of any single power. The United States could not even tolerate the domination of Europe by certain combinations of powers, for example, Russia and France or Russia and Germany or Germany and France. Our whole postwar foreign policy in Europe has been inspired by this understanding. One might say that American policy, after a brief period of false hope that the wartime alliance with the Soviet Union would be continued in the postwar era, has followed the grand strategy which we adopted in World War II. We fought in both the Atlantic and the Pacific theaters of war with the two areas competing for preferential allocation of American and British resources in arms and men. The decision to give priority to the European theater was the most important decision in the grand strategy of World War II. It influenced the course

[22] The following three paragraphs are taken from Hans Speier, "Deutschlands Stellung in der amerikanischen Aussenpolitik," *Wehrkunde,* Munich, February, 1966, pp. 59-71; where the argument is discussed more fully.

and the phasing of the world struggle to Churchill's satisfaction, and, occasionally, to MacArthur's chagrin.

After the war the United States broke away from the time-honored tradition of its foreign policy. Instead of avoiding entangling alliances in peacetime it not only assisted Western Europe economically on a very large scale in order to brace it against Soviet expansionism, but also helped to form NATO, an entangling alliance if there ever was one, and stationed large American forces in Europe. Thus Europe remained the primary theater of the political, economic, and military engagement of the United States in the postwar period.

At this point, a few observations on German policy and attitudes toward the war in Vietnam are in order.

In the spring of 1964 the Germans were asked to render some military aid in the fight against the Viet Cong, and as the size of American forces in Vietnam has increased, new U.S. suggestions for German participation in the fighting have been made, for example, by Senator Stennis of Mississippi.[23] The Federal Republic has refused to offer even as much as a token of such aid. It has confined itself to diplomatic and economic support of the U.S. effort in Vietnam. The Federal Republic is the only Western country other than the United States that has embarked upon a world-wide program of economic aid.[24] In Asia the Federal Republic is one of the seven non-Asian members contributing to the Asian Development Bank. Although not a member of the United Nations, West Germany is also one of the more than twenty countries participating in the United Nations Mekong Committee, which coordinates the international effort to help through the Mekong River Project millions of people in Laos, Cambodia, Vietnam, and Thailand. In Vietnam itself the Federal Republic contributes nonmilitary aid to the government in Saigon. On various occasions, however, the Federal Republic has resisted active involvement in military conflicts between NATO members—as on Cyprus—or in any war outside the NATO area, as in the Congo or in Vietnam. The Germans believe that they have good reasons for doing so. They fear that such involvement would provide Communist propaganda with a powerful argument against the Federal Republic. At present all Communist governments, no matter how much their ties with Moscow have been loosened or cut, accuse the Federal Republic of disturbing the peace, of being menacingly militaristic and belligerent, and Germany's participation in any fighting might lend credence to the validity of this accusation. Nor is it unlikely that even in the free world the appearance of West German soldiers in the Mediterranean, Africa, or Asia would revive memories of Germany's past under Hitler and create hostility to the Federal Repub-

[23] For criticism of Senator Stennis' remarks cf. *Die Zeit*, February 4, 1966.

[24] George C. McGhee, "The Roots of American Foreign Policy," *Bulletin*, the Department of State, January 10, 1966, p. 52.

lic. Still other reasons explain German reluctance to participate in anti-Communist wars outside the NATO area. The appearance of West German soldiers in South Vietnam or of military aid in that war-torn country might lead to corresponding East German efforts in support of the Viet Cong or of North Vietnam. This would be tantamount to German fratricide on Asian soil and might have the most serious repercussions in Europe.

French and German policies on Vietnam differ. The President of France defies U.S. policy in Asia as well as Europe and ever since his last election campaign has expressed concern that France might be drawn into a world war by reckless U.S. policies in Asia or elsewhere outside the NATO area.[25]

By contrast, the West German government supports U.S. policy in Vietnam and has never failed to understand that the defense against Communist aggression is indivisible. For example, at the NATO Ministerial Council meeting in December 1965, the government of the Federal Republic declared that it considered the military defense of South Vietnam by the United States against Communist aggression to be necessary until the independence of South Vietnam is assured through negotiations and free elections. Indeed, if the United States were to withdraw ignominiously from Vietnam, it is likely that no European country would react more adversely to such retreat than West Germany, and no city with greater dejection than Berlin. This is so because nowhere in Europe has the danger of Communist aggression been experienced with greater concern than in West Germany and in West Berlin.

If the war in Vietnam has caused moral concern and fear in Germany, it has not been the government which has given voice to these feelings, but primarily some journalists, professors, and students. While German opposition to American policy in Vietnam is neither as widespread nor as vocal as it has been in the United States, some student demonstrations have occurred in Munich and elsewhere. On February 6, even Berlin, which owes its continued freedom to American protection, was the scene of a small demonstration of students who tore down the American flag in front of the America House.[26]

These are actions to which perhaps not too much political importance ought to be attached. But the Germans are indeed in a quandary regarding Vietnam. On the one

[25] At his press conference of February 21, De Gaulle said, "... while the possibility that a world war might break out in Europe is receding, at least to a certain extent, there are other conflicts in which America is involved in other parts of the world—as once in Korea, yesterday in Cuba, and today in Vietnam—that could escalate to a general conflagration, in which Europe whose strategy in NATO is the same as America's would be automatically implicated, even if it had not wanted it." (*The New York Times*, February 22, 1966.)

[26] Two days later, in a blizzard of snow, a much larger counterdemonstration was held at the same spot.

hand, they do not want to be drawn into active participation in the fighting. A debate in the *Bundestag*—the West German Parliament—held as recently as January 12 of this year, made it clear how profoundly disturbed the Germans are about the possibility of such participation. They want their support confined to economic and humanitarian aid; for example, they have provided a hospital ship for Vietnam, but deputies in the *Bundestag* demanded binding declarations from Mr. Schröder, the Foreign Minister, that no single German soldier, whether in uniform or in civilian clothes, would be sent to Vietnam.

On the other hand, the Germans fear that any failure to support the United States militarily in Vietnam may provide justification for the United States to withdraw American troops from Europe. As a German commentator put it recently, "Washington wants to issue an order to march to Vietnam, not to German troops, but to American troops that are stationed in Germany."[27]

The issue of an American troop withdrawal is a highly divisive one in German domestic policy. The majority of West Germans would undoubtedly suffer a psychological shock if American units were withdrawn from Germany on a large scale, because such a move would be understood as the onset of renewed American isolationism leaving the Germans exposed to Soviet pressure. Some other Germans, however, like former Defense Minister Franz Josef Strauss, have openly advocated just such a withdrawal, perhaps in the hope that it would entail either closer French-German relations or that it would give the Federal Republic a basis for insisting on an improvement of its own position in NATO. For example, the Germans could conceivably demand that their own forces be made as independent of NATO as are the contingents of other NATO powers, which in an emergency have temporarily withdrawn certain forces from NATO for use under national authority. The Germans have not had this privilege. Conceivably, they might want to use American troop withdrawals to argue more forcefully with their allies about nuclear strategy or about lifting some of the restrictions that apply at present to German access to nuclear arms.

The Federal Republic was the first country in the world which pledged not to produce atomic, biological, and chemical weapons. This pledge, made in 1954, was one of the prices that West Germany had to pay—and paid at the time without hesitation—for the political resurrection of its sovereignty and for membership in Western collective defense. The pledge was subject to certain restrictions. For example, it pertained only to the production of nuclear weapons on German soil, not to the production elsewhere, nor to the purchase of nuclear arms. More importantly, it was a pledge made to West Germany's allies and not to neutrals or adversaries.

Now for several years it has been a major aim of American policy to halt the

[27] Theo M. Loch in *Bayern-Kurier*, February 19, 1966.

further spread of nuclear weapons by international agreement. The language in which this aim of American policy has been stated and justified by some high-ranking officials, such as Mr. William Foster, has given rise to deep concern in some German circles. It has appeared to them that the United States, faced with Soviet opposition to the multilateral force, might be ready to abandon the search for a way of sharing nuclear power in NATO in order to obtain Soviet agreement to a treaty on non-proliferation. The official German position is that the Federal Republic would sign a *general* agreement only if it were accompanied by progress on German reunification. While it may be said that the adoption of this position does not betray much prudence, since it may arouse anti-German feelings in Western Europe, it does not violate any international agreements.

IV

The Soviet Union has applied so-called *salami* tactics against the Western powers in Berlin, reducing their position over the years by taking away a slice at a time; De Gaulle, too, has followed such *salami* tactics with regard to NATO. In the past few years France has withdrawn "its Mediterranean and Atlantic Fleets from NATO; assigned to NATO only small French air and ground forces (about 60,000 men); refused to permit non-French-controlled nuclear weapons on French territory; withdrawn French naval personnel from certain high NATO command posts; not accepted the 1962 NATO Council guidelines for the use of nuclear weapons; not committed itself to consult with its allies on the use of these weapons in contingencies of an ambiguous nature; announced its refusal to participate in the 1966 FALLEX Program; not participated in the Ten Nations Special Nuclear Committee."[28] Most recently the General has served formal notice that he regards the presence of foreign military personnel and bases in peacetime on French soil as incompatible with the sovereignty of France and that he will also withdraw French troops from integrated NATO commands. He hopes to enjoy the benefits of American nuclear protection "regardless of what he does or what happens to the Atlantic Alliance."[29] We shall hear much about the political consequences of De Gaulle's action in the next few months. Probably the interests of the other members of NATO in collective defense will continue to prevail with or without French participation. In this connection it is useful to remember that the United States, the United Kingdom, and Germany together account for about 86 per cent of the defense expenditures of all NATO countries; the contribution of France is 6 per cent; that of all other remaining NATO countries combined is 8 per cent.

[28] *The Atlantic Alliance—Basic Issues.* A study of the Subcommittee on National Security and International Operations (chairman, Henry M. Jackson), February 18, 1966, p. 7.
[29] *Ibid.*

It is possible, however, to look at these figures in a different light by comparing the American contribution with that of all other NATO countries. The ratio is about seven to three, or, in absolute figures estimated for 1964–1965 in billions of dollars, roughly about fifty to twenty. Now twenty billion dollars spent for defense by the European members of NATO (including Great Britain) is a very sizable amount, and one might well ask why it should not be possible for Europe—though not for France alone—to attend to her own security without American help. Andrew Marshall has recently examined this question more closely. He comes to the conclusion that the European countries "are not now, nor are they likely in the near future to be, nearly able to defend themselves against potential maximum Soviet and Warsaw Pact aggression. . . . Their contribution to their own self-defense is well below what in principle it could be. However, the constraints, inefficiencies, and conflicting objectives which have limited their past ability to produce forces adequate for their collective self-defense are unlikely to change rapidly in the future. Many of the causes are built into the European situation: the division of effective decision-making among the twelve nations; the attendant high overhead costs of their military establishment; the political and economic forces within each of the nations which lead to the failure of coordinated production and logistic support operation; the historical attachment in many of the countries to universal military training programs, etc."[30]

Some Frenchmen have expressed the opinion that the French nuclear force is able to protect the security of Western Germany, even if NATO in its present form were to disintegrate. Often this opinion has been associated with the notion that the American commitment to come to the aid of Western Europe, if necessary with nuclear arms, is unreliable and incredible, given the Soviet ability to kill many millions of Americans in a nuclear war, even if Russian missiles and bombs were to strike second. A few Germans have echoed this opinion, although it must be stressed that they speak only for a small minority of their countrymen. In a survey taken in June 1965, only eleven out of a hundred West Germans expressed the view that the Federal Republic should cooperate more closely with France on armament and defense, while sixty-three felt that it should cooperate more closely with the United States; (26 per cent of the sample were "undecided").[31] The West German government, as well as the large majority of the West Germans, knows that France is unable to take the place of the United States in deterring Soviet aggression. Indeed, without U.S. participation only a politically united Western Europe, with a European nuclear force based on the resources of such a united Europe, could conceivably hold its

[30] A. W. Marshall, "Determinants of NATO Force Posture" (P-3280, January, 1966, The RAND Corporation), pp. 20–21.

[31] Erich Peter Neumann, "Probleme unseres Frankreich-Bildes," *Die politische Meinung,* September, 1965, p. 28.

own against Soviet nuclear power—sometime in the future. Europe is not politically unified, however, and bringing its nuclear armament up to par with that of the Soviet Union would require after political unification at least a decade of concerted effort at the expense of other military and economic tasks. In speaking of such a possibility we are coming very close to describing a utopian state of affairs. Thus, the American nuclear deterrent remains indispensable for the protection of the security interests of West Germany and Western Europe.

For Germany, De Gaulle's action against NATO has created many serious new problems; I shall refer to only a few of them.

1) At present France has allocated to NATO two divisions that are stationed on German soil; a few French aircraft squadrons are also integrated into NATO and operate from German territory. What is to become of these forces? If De Gaulle is consistent he will either have to pull these forces back to France or try to conclude a special agreement with the Federal Republic permitting him to leave them on German territory. He has invoked French sovereignty in order to deny such a privilege to American and Canadian contingents in France. Will the Federal Republic be less concerned about its sovereignty than De Gaulle is about that of France? Chancellor Erhard quickly indicated that the possibility of a Franco-German bilateral agreement, which De Gaulle seemed to be seeking, would have to be studied—a polite way of saying that the West German government did not necessarily wish to conclude such an agreement. Negotiations between France and the Federal Republic will begin in May 1966. In the meantime, it has become clear that Bonn will negotiate with Paris only on the basis of decisions reached by all other NATO allies; these decisions will be made on proposals formulated by a working group in Bonn, on which the United States, Great Britain, and the Federal Republic are represented.

2) At present France, the United Kingdom, and the United States are represented on the Standing Group of NATO. The Federal Republic is not. Apparently France wishes to maintain its position on the Standing Group. But can one expect West Germany to put up with continued exclusion from it, while she furnishes the largest contingent of conventional forces to the Alliance and after France has so drastically repudiated her commitments? In some other respects as well the Federal Republic may press for the removal of existing inequities in NATO, which she has borne in the past.

3) In his letter to President Johnson of March 7, 1966, General de Gaulle pointed out, "Unless there are changes in the fundamental bases of relations between East and West during the next three years, [France] will in 1969 (when a NATO member may denounce the treaty) and later be resolved, as she is today, to fight on the side of her allies in case one of them is the object of *unprovoked aggression.*"[32]

[32] Text in *The New York Times*, March 25, 1966; italics added.

Other official French spokesmen have followed De Gaulle in predicating the *casus foederis* on "unprovoked aggression." In April Allied delegations in Paris were said to "have begun with studies" to determine the practical meaning of this phrase.[33] It can be found also in the French-Soviet mutual assistance treaty of 1935, signed for France by the then Prime Minister Pierre Laval. It cannot be found, however, in the North Atlantic Treaty of April 4, 1949, which in Article 5 stipulates instead, "The Parties agree that an *armed attack* against one or more of them in Europe or North America shall be considered an attack against them all . . ."[34] An obligation predicated on armed attack differs considerably from one predicated on "unprovoked aggression"; the latter kind of attack would be a matter of interpretation, whereas the former would be a matter of fact. Thus De Gaulle decided not only to dissolve bilateral and multilateral agreements between France and her allies concluded in implementation of the Treaty of 1949 but also to change unilaterally the commitment France has under that Treaty.

The way the American government decides to deal with this far-reaching challenge will inevitably influence future German foreign policy. In this crisis, appearances to the contrary notwithstanding, anything less than an energetic assertion by the United States of the Atlantic interest as defined in the Treaty of 1949 may in the long run lead to a reorientation of German foreign policy at U.S. expense.

4) It is possible that De Gaulle's action will serve as a justification in certain American circles for advocating the withdrawal of American troops from Europe. Senator Mansfield has already spoken in this vein. As has been pointed out, such a move would have seriously unsettling effects in Germany. In fact, even the temporary withdrawal of fifteen thousand American troops from Germany in April 1966, appeared ill timed and alarming to the Germans.

5) What is to become of the French presence in West Berlin? It is true, the contingents of the three main Western powers are in Berlin not as NATO forces, but as a result of an agreement among the Soviet Union, the United States, and the United Kingdom, which the French were later permitted to join. Even so, it might sooner or later appear to Germany (or to other powers) as an anomaly for a French force to remain in West Berlin, particularly if France should be refused permission to maintain her divisions in West Germany or if she were to move politically closer to the Soviet Union.

6) What is to become of the Western effort toward the reunification of Germany? Again, this effort is not directly affected by De Gaulle's action against NATO, but

---

[33] *Die Welt*, April 19, 1966.

[34] *NATO: Facts about the North Atlantic Treaty Organization* (Paris: NATO Information Service, 1965), p. 211; italics added.

from the German point of view the solidarity of the Western powers with regard to this issue is an indispensable prerequisite for any future negotiations with the Soviet Union. De Gaulle's defection from NATO cannot fail to strain the political solidarity among the major Western allies on issues other than collective defense. This lesson cannot be lost on the Germans and may induce them to reconsider the approaches to reunification that are open to them. For the time being, it may subtly strengthen the appeal of neutralism.

7) The French have developed their nuclear force without being checked by the other six countries of the Western European Union. Article 3 of Protocol No. III of the Paris Treaties of October 23, 1954, pertaining to the control of armaments, stipulated, however:

> When the development of atomic, biological and chemical weapons in the territory on the mainland of Europe of the High Contracting Parties who have not given up the right to produce them has passed the experimental stage and effective production of them has started there, the level of stocks that the High Contracting Parties concerned will be allowed to hold on the mainland of Europe shall be decided by a majority vote of the Council of Western European Union.

Sometime in the future a West German government may conceivably call attention to the fact that the German declaration of October 3, 1954, not to undertake the manufacture on its territory of atomic, biological, and chemical weapons was taken note of and agreed with in Article 1 of the same Protocol by the same High Contracting Parties that failed to apply Article 3 of that Protocol to France. It is of some interest that this discriminatory use of the Protocol was mentioned in the *Bundestag* debate of March 17, 1966, by Fritz Erler, the parliamentary leader of the Social Democrats, in the course of a criticism of De Gaulle's policy. It is conceivable that some day some other German may use the same argument not so much against France as in favor of Germany.

To date, more than twenty years after the end of military hostilities in World War II, there is no stable order in Europe. None has existed since the end of World War I. The American presence in Western Europe, established after the end of World War II, helped to safeguard peace and order in Europe, but peace has never been completely assured and hence order has never been stable. The symbol of Europe's instability has been the division of the Continent with divided Germany in its midst. While De Gaulle may have succeeded in ringing down the curtain on a period of postwar history, it may be doubted that he has taken a constructive step toward achieving political order in Europe.

Western Europe, Eastern Europe, and the Soviet Union

FRITZ ERLER

That the wartime coalition against Hitler had already disintegrated in 1944 became clearly visible in 1945 when it came to making the major decisions over Europe and Germany. The Soviets then had taken over Eastern Europe and a good part of Germany. Soviet troops in Poland and elsewhere were the deterrent to free elections, which originally had been promised to those nations when the war should come to an end. In Czechoslovakia there were no Soviet troops, but that country was governed by a coalition in which the Communists held the important positions of Defense Minister and the Minister of the Interior—commanding the police. On the basis of such a situation, where Communist power was already strongly invested, Czechoslovakia also went the way of the other Eastern European countries and disappeared behind the Iron Curtain. This experience helps explain why the United States is sensitive to coalition governments with Communists where the Communists are in powerful positions, a situation that might arise also in Viet Nam.

Europe of course has had experiences of another kind with coalition governments including Communists, for example, in France after 1945, or in Austria. But the conditions there differed from those in Eastern Europe. The Communists were part of a set-up in which the other parties had strong support derived from free elections. This strength made it possible to maintain freedom, but both in France and in Austria the presence of American forces in Europe also provided protection against a minority party's taking over power against the will of the nation involved.

The year 1948 witnessed the blockade of Berlin and the Communist take-over at Prague. These two events furnished the basic impetus for the founding of NATO—the Western response to the aggressiveness of Soviet policy in Europe. However, the formation of the Atlantic Alliance and of its organizational framework followed another very important development: the Marshall Plan for the recovery of European economy, not only through American aid, but also through good advice. Our American friends said to the Europeans: please pool your resources, see what you can do for each other, find out what you need for the rebuilding of Europe after you have pooled your resources, and then we Americans will foot the bill. So it happened—with American help and European cooperation in the framework of what was called then the OEEC (Organization for European Economic Cooperation).

Later it became known as OECD (Organization for Economic Cooperation and Development), when it grew into an organization for European cooperation together with America and Canada in fields of development outside Europe. With the help of American aid and through good organization, the economic power of Europe was restored and the standard of living was raised, thus eliminating a natural basis for Communist infiltration, since human suffering is the best aid to Communist propaganda.

If a prize were to be awarded for creating European unity, for making an effort toward European integration, I should pick two recipients. The first would be Marshal Stalin, because without Soviet pressure Europe probably would not have made this great effort to unite. The second would be General Marshall of the United States of America, because without his great concept of aid the Europeans would not have discovered the need to pool their resources. We in the European movement have recognized these two so different services rendered to European unity, but at the same time we have held it necessary to develop European unity from motivations other than either external pressure or advice by a good friend. We felt that there should be also native sources in Europe for developing a greater sense of unity, based on enlightened self-interest and drawing on the great history of this continent which has laid the basis of our Western civilization.

Now, the success story of cooperation and integration in Europe starts in the economic field. There is first the Common Market: the European Economic Community; the Coal and Steel Community; and Euratom, the organization for the peaceful use of atomic energy on the European scale. The looser organizations like the OECD, on the other hand, have far more members, including not only the six countries of the Common Market—France, Italy, Netherlands, Belgium, Luxembourg, and West Germany (these are in the inner group of the six)—but also a larger area, ranging from the North Cape down to Greece and Turkey, including also Portugal.

Another organization, which does not include Portugal, however, is the Council of Europe. The Council is mostly a very interesting forum for the exchange of ideas. Most leading political figures in Europe know each other because they have been members of this parliamentary assembly at one time or other. The Council of Europe has accomplished much in a series of conventions which, not only binding the governments but also leaving their imprint in national laws, have helped to harmonize legislation in different fields all over Europe. The most important of these is the convention on human rights. Contrary to the declaration of human rights in the United Nations, the Council of Europe's convention on rights can be enforced. The United Nations created a declaration; but if the right is violated, you can't do anything but protest. In the Council of Europe there exist a commission to investigate violations and a court to adjudicate such cases. Two examples of where this machinery of the Council of Europe has helped to solve political disputes will suffice: the Saar question between Germany and France, and Cyprus, which had won its independence after having been a disputed area between Britain and Greece. Acceptance of this convention on human rights is a kind of entrance card to membership in the club of free nations in Europe, a test which makes it understandable that countries like Portugal, Spain, and Yugoslavia, which are interested in a closer cooperation in the economic field nevertheless cannot become members of the European Communities and of this Assembly as long as they cannot choose, by general free elections, their members to the European Parliamentary Assembly. This needs to be said because there is a good deal of talk on the relations to be established between Spain and the other countries of Europe. We desire such good relations partly so that the Spanish people should not suffer on account of their present form of government, which excludes them, for example, from the economic advantages of close ties to the European Common Market. It is up to Spain herself, however, to create the prerequisite for full membership in the organizations mentioned and also to establish political freedom for her people.

Some countries which are now full members in the Council of Europe in the past have been merely associates and before that only observers, because they are neutral in the military sense (Switzerland, Austria). Now a new observer has joined the assembly—an impressive one, a very interesting country, though it is not quite within the geographical area of Europe: Israel. I welcome the presence of Israel because it shows that that country really wishes to be a member of the European family of nations.

The cooperating, organized European Communities have had to face quite a series of problems during the last years. Great Britain, Denmark, Norway, and Ireland applied for membership. It seemed desirable to include as associates certain other countries which did not deem it wise to become full members. We also wanted the Communities to obtain a still more democratic structure by giving more rights to the parliamentary assembly—for example, with respect to passing the budget, which it cannot do now—and by composing this parliamentary assembly through direct elections from the European electorates rather than by delegation from the national parliaments of the various member states. All these efforts failed. Then we tried to strengthen the autonomy of the EEC, so that it would not follow the instructions of the component national governments but would be guided by a kind of European executive board, though not a government (since its power is not large enough): a European Commission under President Hallstein. We tried to give the Commission more powers so as to have an organization which thinks of the urgent problems of the day in terms of the European common interest and not merely in terms of the national interest of nation states. This effort failed likewise.

Another point is that we believe, and this will become a necessity, that the European Communities should extend their jurisdiction over other activities, and not limit themselves to only the economic field. Already today there is a definite tie between economy and foreign policy. Trade policy, for one, cannot be made without reference to foreign policy at large. Trade with Eastern Europe, for example, is of political importance; consequently there is a certain degree of common policy within the European Community of the Six on this issue, but this unity should be widened to embrace foreign policy in general and, furthermore, to create a situation in which the European states would pool their defense efforts within the framework of NATO so as to act as one partner in NATO and not as six different ones. Another very important issue is the relationship existing between the European Community and the U.S.A. Should the Community be a partner, as President Kennedy wished it to be, or is there perhaps a growing rivalry between the economic power of the rebuilt Europe and that of the United States? This conflict between partnership and rivalry is reflected in the very difficult discussions about the Kennedy Round—that great offer to lower the tariffs all over the globe by about 50 per cent in order to further the development of world trade. The debate has shown, however, that, unfortunately, protectionism is still alive in Europe, most plainly visible in the field of agriculture.

Some plead for a high degree of self-sufficiency in agriculture in Europe, while others, such as the Bonn Government as well as my own party, favor a liberal trade policy as laid down in the treaty. The Federal Republic of Germany is an important exporter, but one cannot export on a large scale without giving other countries a chance to earn the money needed to pay for what they import. Here is the difference between the French position and that of the others. But the German farming communities are also interested in protection. Now, it is obvious that in most of the industrial countries of the world farm policy has little to do with economics. But rather it is tied to the problem of social welfare for the farming community, and therefore all these countries face the problem of paying subsidies which stimulate production, and of then paying more subsidies to export the surpluses. This is a problem facing Europe now—it is a rather new one for the Germans, who in trying to strike a balance between a liberal trade policy and agricultural protectionism are just following the example set by the United States. We recognize, of course, that changes of policy—which are inevitable—will require certain adjustments. They may call for different kinds of jobs and vocational retraining; they might produce hardships, as in the case of the coal miners, who virtually have to give up their trade. But we feel that such adjustments inside the European Economic Community, and to world-wide competition, will have to be made in the interest of promoting world trade and of producing goods where they can be most favorably produced for all consumers.

In respect to most of these problems there are differences with the present French government. That government blocked the British entrance into the European Community. An argument which was not officially used, but which could be read in the French press, was that the French essentially regarded the British as not really Europeans but as agents of the United States. More recently this position seems to have undergone a change: at the last ministerial meeting of the Western European Union the French representatives said that they had no objection to British entry into the Common Market. Perhaps this was only an attempt to influence the British elections; but, whatever the purpose may be, I think we should take these French declarations seriously and test them. To go to the conference table and resume the debate on British entry would be all for the good, not only for the British, but also for the European Communities.

The other point is that France is striving for more independence from the United States. (There is a cartoon showing the French President before a map of France; arrows are indicating where the American troops would have to go in order to leave France, and the caption says "This time it is I who will have liberated France.") The underlying basis of the present French policy is the doctrine of the nation-state: it says that only the nation-state is a reality in our time, and that every attempt to pool sovereignty is sheer nonsense. So the General believes, and this is why he is calling the officials of the European Communities "les apatrides"—the men without a fatherland. I consider this charge undeserved, for their fatherland is Europe. They are imbued with a new spirit, they think in larger dimensions than the outmoded nation-state. But here is the basic issue in the current dispute between France and the other countries, both in Europe and in the United States.

Now to the problem of NATO, which is in a crisis. The French want to remain in the Alliance but do not want to take part in the Organization. It is hard to conceive that one can expect to enjoy protection by a defense alliance without contributing to the common defense effort. The desire to be in the Alliance but not in the Organization reminds one of the attempt in the year 1954, when the creation of a European integrated army was under consideration. When it came to the size of the different components to be integrated the French clearly advanced the thesis that the German armed force should be stronger than the Russian but weaker than the French—a goal which would have been difficult to achieve.

If one looks deeply into the problem he finds good grounds for believing that France ought to have another look at the situation and not make decisions too hastily. The problem mainly revolves around foreign bases on French soil. Most of these bases were negotiated bilaterally between France and her partners. The issue therefore has to be argued out between those who have made the agreements. Then, there is the problem of the command structure set up in peacetime for readiness to insure a quick and effective defense in case of necessity. The question here is whether the French withdrawal might not prove detrimental to French security. When the French withdraw their officers from integrated commands and eliminate the NATO headquarters from French soil, they will lose all influence in military planning, which covers the security of France as well as that of other partners.

I believe this crisis could have been foreseen. The position of De Gaulle in regard to the sovereignty theme has been known for years, although the French government never made precise proposals concerning it. Now it has announced unilateral action, and professes to be ready to discuss only the consequences of that action, not the action itself. I think the other partners of the Alliance must bring the discussion back into the framework of the Alliance, and not discuss the vital problems of our survival on a bilateral basis, because to do even this would entail a partial destruction of NATO. I have already mentioned the long list of French interests at stake—the protection provided by the Alliance and by the United States, and the infrastructure on French soil also serving French security needs. For example, if the radar system and the electronic guidance system of the Alliance were no longer available to the French Air Force, De Gaulle might as well junk the Air Force—it would be useless, it would be blind. The stationing of French troops in Germany is a problem affecting the Alliance as a whole and therefore cannot be settled by bilateral arrangements only. The French are no longer an occupying power—they are an ally. The French troops in Germany have a mission within the Alliance. But I also think that France would be interested in having troops in Germany as an additional protection for France and as an instrument of influence on the future of Germany, in which France also has a stake.

Finally, there is the question of the cost of the equipment which has been constructed in France and which has been financed in common—a very interesting list. And while I am not overoptimistic, I do think that if the solidarity of the fourteen can really be maintained, there is a good chance that we can bring back our French partner into a discussion inside NATO. Additional reason for hope resides in the fact that France has not left the NATO Council. The French have said that they want the NATO Council to remain in Paris, and they want to have a seat in that Council. They regard the NATO Council as a part not of the Organization but of the Alliance; therefore, one may hope that the discussion can be continued.

Such has been the situation in the Community of the Six. After the French had played the game of the empty chair for nearly one year the solidarity of the other five brought them back. The crisis has not been overcome by this—it has been postponed; but the essentials of the institutions have been preserved, and I think a similar development appears reasonable also in NATO. Here too is the possibility of a compromise. There are words which frighten the French. One does not need to insist on specific words if one wishes to preserve essentials. If we need a better word, let us look into the dictionary for other expressions than supranational integration; what counts is the real meaning behind the words, not the formulas. Therefore, I think that some face-saving devices are possible, if there is a minimum of good will. Some people have asked if all this was done by President de Gaulle in order to bring a gift to Moscow when he goes there. I do not think so, because such an interpretation underestimates the real Soviet interest. The Soviet interest in De Gaulle is great, as long as he retains a certain nuisance value inside the Alliance. After leaving the Alliance France, as an individual power, would no longer be a very interesting partner for the Soviet Union. In other words, the maintenance of very good relations with France would not be considered a worthwhile objective in Moscow if it entailed the risk of ruining the Soviet effort to maintain, and even improve, good relations with the real power in world affairs—the United States of America. It is obvious that the two great atomic powers are trying their best to avoid a direct confrontation, especially in the nuclear field.

The other point is that the Soviet Union has a certain fear about an exclusive alliance between the United States and Germany. The French move on NATO increases the relative weight of the Federal Republic of Germany and forces Germany and the United States to establish even stronger ties than they had before. This, however, runs directly against Soviet interest. I am not at all convinced, therefore, that De Gaulle is going to get really successful results in Moscow. He will be received as an interesting guest, but I do not believe that events really dangerous and detrimental to the Alliance will follow his visit to Russia.

As for Franco-German relations, the reconciliation between these two nations is one of the great achievements of the post-World War II period, and we should try our best to keep alive this kind of relationship which mainly the young generation of both these countries now maintains. It has developed in such a way that even mistakes by the governments, I believe, cannot destroy the friendship between the nations. The streams of blood released by the disputes between France and Germany should remain a part of past history and should not be allowed to flow again. A preamble to the Franco-German consultation treaty, approved by all parties in the Bundestag, states that we say yes to this friendship and reconciliation but that we do not consider Franco-German friendship an alternative to the European Community and Atlantic solidarity, but simply an aspect of these Communities, which need not weaken our other commitments. My party has a strong, hundred-year-old tradition of working for reconciliation, and we have made sacrifices and lost lives for it at a time when nationalism ravaged both our countries. The idea of a common policy between France and Germany as members of a larger family has always existed, and it was never assumed that one nation would simply impose its will upon the other.

President De Gaulle has said that a real Communist threat no longer exists. Chancellor Adenauer also has ranked the Soviet Union among the peace-loving nations, to the great surprise of his successor. I should not overestimate this statement, for it was meant as a tactical move to embarrass the successor. But we must admit that there have been changes in the Soviet Union herself and in the Eastern bloc. These changes inside the Communist societies are not the cause of their less aggressive foreign policy which we have witnessed since Cuba. The main reason for this development is the existence of a strong Western community and of a joint defense effort. Those who dismantle these elements of Western unity destroy the very instrument which has been created for forcing the Soviet Union into more reasonable behavior. To destroy NATO might easily provoke a revival of aggressiveness on the other side, against Berlin for example. I admit that China has also contributed to the new course of the Soviet Union in foreign policy. The Soviet Union, for once, does not want to be more involved in Vietnam than it is now. But the fight for leadership inside the Communist world limits Soviet flexibility and makes the Soviets quite stubborn on all questions relating to Europe.

What are the changes in the USSR? The terror, the police-state aspect has diminished. There is more confidence in law and correct administration. There is a good deal of economic decentralization. Cultural life has become somewhat freer but restraints are now being imposed again on scientists, writers, and poets. Human nature will enforce more freedom in private life and in the arts and sciences, but only to the extent that this poses no threat to the regime itself. The Soviet Union remains a country ruled by a monopolist party. In such a system quick changes are possible, involving all kinds of surprises, and the nation is never asked about the scope and character of the changes which are ordered from the top. There is no indication of major changes in Soviet policy toward Europe, as best illustrated by Moscow's policy on disarmament. The Soviets are not ready to discuss disarmament as reduction of either atomic weapons or conventional forces—an attitude which is bound to block disarmament altogether. They are unwilling to accept inspection, which alone could assure that an agreement is being kept. In Europe they not only are refusing Germany the right of self-determination, they also are trying to make the division of Germany permanent. And the Soviets have maintained a firm hold on Eastern Europe in all vital foreign-policy questions—even in some internal respects; only in economic affairs is there more freedom.

In Berlin there is no dramatic threat at the moment, but the Communists work patiently, step by step, to undermine the Western positions. Unfortunately, the West yielded to their pressure before when they shouted loudly enough—for example, when it did not allow the authorities of the Federal Republic to be present in West Berlin on the same footing as the authorities of the Communist part of Germany in

East Berlin. This situation should be more equitable, so as to show that Berlin is the capital of all of Germany, and not just a part of the Soviet-occupied territory.

A word about the changes that have taken place in Eastern Europe. These states remain Communist states, but they are making important economic reforms in a novel way. One of my friends, recently back from Warsaw, told me that the Polish economists have found a new definition for their form of socialism: they call socialism the slowest way to capitalism. Cultural developments, with their ups and downs, have been visible in Poland and Hungary. Poland was first in curtailing liberties, and Hungary now is the country having the greatest freedom of expression and of contact with other countries, as in admitting foreign publications. The area where aspirations and independence from Soviet domination are pushed most by the Communist governments is the economic field. The outstanding example here was the fight for greater industrialization in Rumania, a state which has played the Chinese card in order to make the Russians more reasonable—and played it successfully.

What should the West do to encourage this? I think better relations are useful. Trying to disturb the relations between the Eastern European countries and the Soviet Union is useless. There is enough strife in the world already. De Gaulle claims that he is the pioneer in opening the Eastern European countries to Western influence. This just is not true. In fact, he is a "Johnny-come-lately." He vetoed the American attempt, more than eight years ago, to develop better economic and cultural relations with Poland and other European countries. He was the sharpest critic of this scheme. I am quite happy that he now supports the development of closer relations between those countries and other Western countries; and I am also quite happy that the Federal Republic of Germany finally joins in these endeavors too. We are the last to do so, a fact which I regret because we are indeed the closest neighbor of the East. For years my political friends advocated the development of economic relations with the East European states, of cultural exchanges, and of establishing our presence there, so as not to leave these nations exposed only to the Communist propaganda from the regime in East Berlin. Our government was slow in accepting this advice, but in the end it did. Bonn created trade missions; but that was not all. I think that the latest German peace note is a good piece of diplomacy, inasmuch as it makes quite plain our readiness to offer the East European states, if they want them, mutual nonaggression pacts which would bar any resort to force. We are ready to take part even at a world-wide disarmament conference if we are wanted there. We are ready to go far in respect to disarmament arrangements, without which there can be no hope for German reunification, but which cannot be agreements binding Germany alone. For, what happens when one country is singled out and a special status imposed on it was shown by the Weimar Republic, which broke down in part because democratic Germany was discriminated against even by her friends, while the dictator Hitler was later rewarded for blackmailing the West. This error should not be repeated. Only disarmament settlements covering large areas, and including the whole of Germany as well as other countries, are feasible and advisable.

The German government has said that it makes no territorial claims against Czechoslovakia; it has also said that the Polish border is a problem whose solution, as the Allies decided, should be postponed until the peace treaty is made for the whole of Germany. This position we cannot give up. We are willing to discuss the border problem at a conference table, but our Polish neighbors cannot have it both ways. They cannot base their policy on the existence of two independent, sovereign German states, and at the same time ask the one state, which, in that case, would not be Poland's neighbor, for a recognition of the border of a foreign state. If the Poles want to discuss anything it must be the future border between a united Germany and Poland, for only then would the West Germans be neighbors of the Poles. Admittedly Germany started and lost the Second World War. That peace demands its price is understood, but, if so, sacrifices must also bring about unity and self-determination. We cannot afford to play for nothing. We do not have many cards to play, and we want at least to make our friends and others understand that at stake is a valuable asset—one third of the former German territory. It is an area in which centuries of German cultural history have been invested, in whose cities even the stones talk German. This does not mean a claim that everything has to be returned but merely a plea to understanding that a sacrifice of this order cannot be made lightheartedly for nothing. If, for the sake of peace, sacrifices are made, it should be understood how important they are. If we fail to make this clear to the other side now, we shall have to pay yet another bill for the end of the war at the conference table.

The question of diplomatic relations between the Federal Republic of Germany and the East European nations could have been resolved more easily five years ago; I was for such relations, although I recognized that the Hallstein doctrine has a sound core. We have no interest in prompting other governments to establish diplomatic relations with the East German puppet regime. This really would cement the partition of Germany, would make it more permanent. On the other hand I have always had doubts that our threat to break diplomatic relations was the best weapon to stop the recognition of Pankow. It was bound to lay us open to every kind of blackmail, as was seen by the action of the Arab states when we established diplomatic relations with Israel. Therefore, I believe here is a field where we should develop a policy similar to our position in the military sphere: in place of massive retaliation there should be flexible response, which would be better adapted to our diplomatic needs. But we should also insist that the establishment of diplomatic relations should not be contingent on other conditions. We are ready to establish diplomatic relations on such terms. But some of the East European countries have laid down additional requirements, such as our acceptance of an integral part of a German peace settlement without a peace conference, and of a divided Germany. This we cannot do, and for the moment therefore the establishment of diplomatic relations with Eastern Europe is not a very practical proposition. And diplomatic relations, of course, cannot be diplomatic relations between the Federal Republic of Germany and the Soviet-occupied part of the country, for Germany is one country and it cannot have diplomatic relations with itself. All we need is that the administration in East Berlin whose existence we cannot deny, although it has no popular support either in West Germany or on its own side—should try its best to create better human conditions, a bit more freedom of movement, so that human beings should not suffer in yet another way in consequence of the continued partition of the country. That is all; we cannot create diplomatic relations with the Soviet zone; it is not a foreign state.

The main aspects of the future of Germany have to be discussed between the West and the Soviet Union, not with the East German government, because the real problem is how to get rid of it. Since the Ulbricht regime would never discuss its own disappearance, we must discuss with the Soviet Union under what international conditions the solution in the heart of Europe could be achieved. To do so, however, Germany must know that she will not be alone. We need Western solidarity but we need also an understanding on the part of our Eastern neighbors. We have to overcome the existing fear caused by terrible decades in German history. We must banish this fear, for instance, through disarmament. The problem is one of security—against Germany, but also for Germany. The Soviet Union should know, in its own interest, that a united Germany would be a correct, and perhaps even friendly neighbor. It should, therefore, seek to overcome the animosity of a whole nation by ending the partition which it imposes upon it. A united Germany fitted into the framework of a larger Europe would offer, in the economic field, a far greater advantage to the Soviet Union than the profits it can now realize in its part of Germany.

As regards the long-term prospect, I feel that Western Europe will have to develop more unity, that a united Western Europe ought to function as a partner of the United States, one which understands that neither the United States nor Europe can remain independent of each other but that both must work together. It is in the common interest of the two super powers outside Europe to avoid nuclear war. The integration of Europe into the larger framework is an instrument for overcoming the fears others have of Germany. The EEC should develop along those lines, toward a larger Common Market, which includes Britain, a more democratic Common Market, and one that has a better approach to Eastern Europe, especially in regard to the economic and cultural areas and to the political consequences which could flow from these changes. Further changes may appear then—more social justice perhaps in Western Europe, more human freedom on the other side of the Iron Curtain. I hope for both.

On both sides there will then be more similarities, reflecting the common heritage of European history. But the sides will not be identical even though Communism might change its exterior form. Variety has always been at once the weakness and the strength of Europe. It is both a virtue and a vice. We do not want uniformity, but we hope for more unity in recognizing our common history and the values at the basis of that history—even though these values have disappeared from the conscience of many people.

We in Europe have learned the hard way that nationalism does not pay, that the age of the nation-state has passed forever, even though young nations are now entering this stage. They have yet to experience it, while we leave it behind. The time for larger units has come, but partnership between the larger unit in Europe and the United States has to work both ways. It will also transform some aspects of the American nation-state. One cannot recommend to others that it is well to overcome the nation-state without living up to these recommendations oneself. But this is a problem of the future. If Europeans are wishing a more equitable position in relation to her great ally they will have to create the necessary environment. This calls for unity and the will to contribute to the great tasks of our time: to keep the peace, to protect freedom, and to help the developing nations of the world to defeat misery and earn a decent living for all their people through their own efforts. Then and only then can we say that our aspirations are being backed by deeds and not just by claims of past grandeur.

American Interests and Europe's Future

JOHN J. MCCLOY

IT WAS SUGGESTED THAT MY CONTRIBUTION TO THIS SERIES SHOULD CARRY THE title "American Interests and Europe's Future," and some months ago I agreed that it was a timely subject, but I did not anticipate that recent events would make it quite *so* timely. In view of current developments a reappraisal of the status of the Western Alliance and what its future validity is or may be to the United States and to Europe is now painfully appropriate.

From many sides we hear that the conditions which brought the Alliance into being have changed and that new attitudes must be adopted in order to conform to these changes. It is said that the nuclear balance between the Soviet Union and the United States is generally recognized and accepted; that considerable time has elapsed since serious threats have been directed against Berlin; that the Cuban missile crisis is three years old and it is not likely that the Soviet Union will be disposed to attempt another such adventure in the foreseeable future. The conclusion is drawn that a serious Soviet threat to Western Europe or perhaps to the United States no longer exists, and that, accordingly, the defensive systems which were erected to meet that threat should now be fundamentally modified or completely discarded.

This attitude, rather spectacularly put forward by General de Gaulle, is reflected to some degree elsewhere in Europe and is even expressed by certain commentators in the United States. Perhaps because of our heavy preoccupation with our Southeast Asian problems this attitude has not been confronted in the past as frankly, possibly, as it should have been. Consequently, until recently, our attention to European and Atlantic problems has not been brought into as sharp a focus as the importance and the exigency of these problems demanded. It has taken the blunt action of General de Gaulle to compel us and the other members of the Alliance to reëxamine the fundamental validity of our earlier postwar policy and, more specifically, to compel the United States to reappraise its interests in Europe's future.

We are all creatures of our individual experiences. I am bound, therefore, to approach the subject from the point of view of one who was active during significant stages in the development of the policies which resulted in the Western Alliance and the creation of its attendant agencies. Misconceptions can always arise from an exclusively historical approach to the problems of the day. New winds do blow on the Alliance; indeed, the preoccupation with Southeast Asia, of which I have spoken, and other factors need to be related to our present European and Atlantic policy. As a result of developments in the Far East the scope and significance of our foreign policy as a world-wide factor in the preservation of the peace, rather than as a matter of import to Atlantic countries only, has come to be realized to a greater degree than at any other time since the close of World War II. While the role played by the United States since the close of the war in the maintenance of peace and the protection of Western security has been massive, its importance has been accented by the wider geographical evidence of its expression and its effect. It is this accented role which, in some degree at least, stimulated opposing interpretations of the future validity of the Alliance. This is probably only another way of saying that with the advent of the nuclear age any policy with regard to one area of the world is inadequate if it does not recognize and measure the forces which are developing in other parts of the world.

Some historical perspective, as well as a current analysis, may be helpful if the present situation in Europe and our relation to it is to be adequately appraised.

It is not necessary to reach far back into the past to trace the evolvement of our foreign policy from the days of our isolation to the present. So short is the span of our activity on the international stage that one does not need to exceed one lifetime. In that short history one comes across episodes which afford interesting analogies, or at least rough parallels, to our present problems.

The Spanish-American War and John Hay's excursion into Far East affairs with his Open Door Policy in China marked our first real entrance on the international stage as a power (if only then as a third-rate nation). In Barbara Tuchman's latest book I read recently of the fierce debate which took place in this country between the imperialists and the anti-imperialists (the hawks and the doves of those days) and the uproar which broke out over the so-called Philippine Insurrection. In those days, though the Army had no helicopters, jungle war was roughly the same frustrating type as that we have now in Vietnam, with atrocities claimed and committed on both sides. Public opinion was divided then as now: it was "manifest destiny" against isolationism; pacifism against militancy, with many serious-minded people wondering how in the world we had got so deeply committed in those far-off malaria-infested jungles of the Far East.

The writer can recall also the furor during his undergraduate days over President Wilson's expedition to Veracruz. The campus was fiercely divided. We had demonstrations then—we did not wear our hair long but we felt we were "participating" as we marched about and carried signs. I hope I am not claiming too much credit for my generation when I say that we made about as much sense at that time as some of the present-day "participants" think or claim they do now.

More serious events were ahead and my education was interrupted by our entry into World War I. We went off to the wars in France, many of us imbued with a crusader spirit. I felt that I was part of a force whose objective was to make the world safe for democracy. In our present perspective it seems that we did a rather poor job, so far as that long-range objective was concerned, but it was United States resources, energy, and sacrifices which eventually threw the balance in that war and brought about the collapse of the 1914-1918 German effort to subjugate the Western European peninsula.

About twenty years later World War II broke out and again the pursuits of my generation were interrupted by service in another Great War—a war which also had originated in Europe and which Europeans found they could not finish.

The part this country played in World War II needs no recounting here. We threw the balance again, and this time we had to bring our full resources and men to bear across both the Atlantic and the Pacific before it was over. The contribution we made to the successful conclusion of hostilities was so great as to be almost immeasurable. Then came the period of rehabilitation. The Bretton Woods institutions were erected—mainly American-supported and inspired. As president of one of them—the World Bank—and later as a military governor and high commissioner for Germany, and as an administrator of the Marshall Plan, I participated in that American involvement as well.

I recount all this not to bore you with what you already know or with a part of my personal history, which could be duplicated by many others, but solely to relate to the lifetime of a single individual both the speed and the depth of the American involvement in world affairs. From Manila Bay to Vietnam, this nation has moved from its status as a third-rate power, with an almost complete noninvolvement in world affairs, to the position of the indisputably strongest power in the world today, with commitments reaching round the globe.

At the stage of rehabilitation after World War II a major attempt was made to restructure the world on a basis which, it was hoped, would eliminate, or greatly decrease, the likelihood of further world wars and their frightful consequences. The United States had been such a factor in determining the outcome of both World Wars that the part it would play in planning new arrangements became of the utmost importance. A less far-reaching, but still major, attempt had been made after World War I with the establishment of the League of Nations. It suffered from the fragile thought that all the dislocations caused by the War could be made right with German reparations. It came apart with the refusal of the United States to participate in the League, and with the emergence of the hard facts of international economics.

After World War II a new concept, implemented in the institution of the United Nations, with a more realistic and humane approach to economic problems by the Western Allies, and with full United States cooperation and participation, came into being. It promptly became apparent that we were not to have Soviet cooperation in any collective effort to deal with the postwar world. The United Nations machinery, obstructed by Soviet vetoes, proved inadequate to resist Stalin's ambitions in Western Europe and to offset the Soviet refusal to honor the agreements made at Teheran, Yalta, and Potsdam. In this situation the free countries decided to erect a convincing political, economic, and military front behind which the Western European peninsula and the British Isles could recover their strength and preserve the political and individual values for which the Allies had fought so long and so hard. This would provide for the defense of the West but it could also serve as the base upon which constructive steps toward disarmament and arms control and the preservation of peace in a nuclear era could be effected with the Communist World. Such a front was created, and, though it was made possible in large part through American design and resources, it had the strong support and stimulation of all the free European countries, but especially of the French government of the time and its leaders.

In retrospect I see this period as marked by foreign policy on an heroic scale. The fact that during this period of disillusionment over Soviet intransigence the United States made to the Soviet Union and to the countries which subsequently became satellites of the Soviet Union an offer of economic aid comparable to that made to our other Allies accents the enlightened character of American policy. The policy was farsighted even though the offer was peremptorily refused by the Soviets, and, under Soviet pressure, by the satellites as well.

The policy brought large dividends, however, in terms of the rehabilitation of Europe and the preservation of the peace. It was the era of the Marshall Plan, the creation of NATO, the genesis of the Common Market, the defense of Berlin, the defense of Greece, the reorientation of Germany and Japan. Though greatly stimulated by the breakdown of cooperation between the Soviet Union and the Western Allies and by the deliberate plan of the Soviet Union to effect Russo-Communist domination over Western Europe, the policy was not a mere counter to those forces. It had a constructive and affirmative aspect as well. Its very form stimulated the thinking which gave rise to the Coal and Steel Community, Euratom, and the Common Market. In essence it called for a collective effort—economic, political, and military—on the part of those European nations, including France and Germany, whose rivalries and periodical attempts to dominate Europe had brought about a succession of wars culminating in the holocausts of the twentieth century.

Implicit in this farsighted policy was the belief, indeed the deep conviction, that the security and welfare of Europe was a matter of vital concern to the United States and to its future. We had become involved in two World Wars started in Europe and we had invested enormous quantities of our resources, energies, and blood for the liberation and rehabilitation of Europe. Similarity of points of view, common at-

tachment to the principles of representative government, the importance of Europe as a center of industrial, cultural, and scientific achievement, historic ties, increased speed of communication—all tended to align and emphasize our common security interests with those of Europe. In this respect our policymakers found their views supported by the thoughtful opinion of the country as a whole.

Two new and significant elements became a part of the new structure. The first was the willingness of the United States to commit itself from the outset to the purposes of the Atlantic Alliance, both in peace and in war. This element was spectacularly demonstrated by the actual presence in Europe of United States troops in force. This practically insured their immediate involvement in the case of any attack on the European continent. The other was the inclusion of Germany in a Western Alliance on a basis of equal partnership. A third element collateral to the Alliance as such perhaps should also be mentioned. It was the policy which led to the creation of a common European economic community. For centuries Germany, or at least Germans, had been suspended between East and West, dangerously swinging between them, much like a cannon loose on a sailing ship. The new concept was to contain the strength and energies of these talented and vigorous people in a larger common purpose, namely, the preservation of European and Western values in a background of peace secured by the Alliance and with the shared responsibilities provided for by the North Atlantic Treaty Organization.

The Atlantic structure was threatened and indeed tested shortly after it was erected. The Soviet Union considered it (shortsightedly, I believe) to be hostile to its interests. The external attacks upon it, however, tended to give it strength, and, to date, the structure must be accounted a great success. The combination of American nuclear power, American commitments, and the renewed prosperity of Europe, stimulated by American economic aid and consolidated by the revived talents and common genius of the Europeans themselves, has produced a sense of European security and well-being. This from the outset has been the objective of American policy.

Another aspect of the NATO concept worthy of remark is the general sense of security it has given to the neutrals who have remained outside the NATO organization, for example, the Swiss, the Swedes, and the Austrians. A substantial element of public opinion, even among the Eastern Europeans, has recognized in NATO a basis for the greater freedom enjoyed among the satellites since its creation. Paradoxically, it is this over-all success of policy rather than the external attacks upon it which has now brought the present challenge to its continuance.

The challenge now thrown down poses a serious question for the United States and the remaining Allies as to the continued significance of NATO, as such, in the collective effort to preserve the peace of the postwar world. NATO is not in itself the full and only expression of the collective effort, but it undoubtedly symbolizes the whole concept. Its intent was to do more than create a series of alliances all to take effect on the outbreak of war. By establishing a strong defensive front based on forward planning, integrated command, and common installations, NATO has served to discourage a breach of the peace.

It is now clear that General de Gaulle is determined to rid France (if not Europe) of these aspects of NATO on the ground that not only is the need, in terms of a Soviet threat, removed, but also that France requires greater independence and flexibility of position than she feels is available to her as a member of NATO. The latter consideration, perhaps, rather than the former, mainly motivates him. Though modification of NATO is no longer a subject for discussion, according to the General, he has declared that France adheres to the Alliance on a come-hostilities basis. Incidentally, he has introduced a new term, in so far as NATO is concerned, on which to condition France's participation even on such a basis. It is the phrase "unprovoked aggression." It is difficult to assume that this was merely an inadvertent alteration in the commitment language of the NATO Treaty.

As definite as General de Gaulle's intent now appears to be, some puzzling problems and contradictions in his position remain.

There is, first, the inherent contradiction involved in the acceptance of the ultimate benefits and security of the Alliance while discarding the burdens or responsibilities which all the other partners accept as the best means of giving reality to their security objectives. Can an Alliance be said to have real meaning if any member or members are able to act unilaterally in determining their obligations and commitments under it?

Secondly, the General and his adherents have questioned the credibility of the American commitments in a nuclear-powered world. The consequences of nuclear devastation are so great, the argument runs, that one cannot rely on American willingness to come to the aid of Europe in case of attack or threatened attack. Yet at the same time the General insists on the withdrawal of the most convincing guarantee of American participation from the outset of any hostilities, namely, the presence of American troops in France in peace time. The presence of American troops elsewhere in Europe, while not for France to determine, must also be fundamentally contrary to French policy. It would be difficult for France to adopt a policy, or for her Allies to understand it if she did, under which, while doubting the credibility of the American commitment and insisting on the withdrawal of American forces from French soil, she still would seek to have United States troops stationed elsewhere in Europe as the guarantee of timely United States intervention from which France would benefit.

Perhaps nothing can be done to make the United States commitments credible to a skeptical France. Though American troops stationed in Europe may not be convincing or adequate enough to induce France to refrain from building a supplementary nuclear force of her own, it is difficult to follow the reasoning which would insist on removing the most convincing guarantee of prompt American response imaginable at least as long as the main defense of France and Europe is not the French *force de frappe* but the American nuclear deterrent.

The General has also argued, in derogation of the American commitment to Europe, that American intervention in the two World Wars arrived belatedly and that only after severe dislocations and destruction had been visited upon the nations and peoples did the United States seek to assist. This may be arguable, even though the liberation of France was accomplished in each instance, but surely it is now no basis for disparaging the very design which seeks to avoid a belated entry. The United States had no pre-existing treaty obligations to intervene in either World War I or World War II, yet without such obligations it did so. Today not only has the United States joined an alliance of mutual assistance but the alliance is supported by troop guarantees which give almost unprecedented reality to its commitments. This would seem to be the most that any one nation, in good conscience, could do to insure action under the treaty.

If, with all this, France does not feel that it can rely on American commitments to respond to an attack or threat of attack on France, one must question whether the Alliance, from the stated French point of view, has validity without those guarantees. If the argument is that France, not being able to depend on the American commitment, must possess a *force de frappe* capable of triggering off a nuclear war at any time France feels it is necessary to do so, thereby inducing or threatening an immediate nuclear attack on the United States, the value of the Alliance is questionable from the American point of view.

Another paradox is the likely effect any break-up of NATO will have upon Germany and her position in the Alliance. France insists that Germany shall not have nuclear weapons; she has opposed the MLF (Multilateral Force), which was designed as a common sharing by Germany and other nonnuclear allies of nuclear security. She has insisted that foreign troops on French soil are an affront to French sovereignty but that French troops stationed on German territory do not carry such an implication for German sovereignty. Yet, if French troops are to remain in Germany they can stay only on the basis of invitation and consent, precisely as American troops and American installations are presently in France. Troops on foreign soil, if not as allies of an operating force in time of war, or as a result of conquest, must be there by some arrangement. Apart from the special position of Berlin, no other foreign troops are on German soil except as part of NATO and all are subject to such integration as NATO involves. If continued presence of foreign troops under NATO integration is an impairment of French sovereignty, how is it possible to maintain that an agreement to permit French troops not under NATO to remain on German soil does not involve a similar impairment of the sovereignty of the Federal Republic of Germany? If it is argued that French troops can remain in Germany under an occupation status or some remnant of it, one can only suggest that this is an indignity that could only tend to contribute ill feeling and needless irritation to an already nervously conditioned Europe.

The equal-partner aspect of NATO was a deliberate determination to reverse the discriminatory provisions of the post-World War I settlement, which did attempt to relegate Germany to a secondary power on the Continent, vis-à-vis France. In the last analysis, it is for Germany to make the decision on the position she wishes to occupy in Europe, but it would be understandable if she vigorously resisted any renewed attempt to relegate her to a secondary position in Europe after receiving so many assurances of her equal status for the future. Yet another alternative which the French action makes possible also is not desirable. The withdrawal of France from NATO at this point certainly tends to create a situation which one would suppose France would not relish, that is, a larger strategic position for Germany in the Alliance, and indeed in Europe, than the NATO structure contemplated.

At least, until recently, General de Gaulle sought the adherence of Germany to his ambitions for France and the future of Europe. He succeeded, it seems, in enlisting the influence of Former Chancellor Adenauer and others to his objectives. It had been the consistent American policy to stimulate a rapprochement between France and Germany. The absence of good relations between them had proved disastrous both for them and for us. All could wholeheartedly applaud if, at long last, rapprochement between France and Germany was in prospect, but too soon it became clear that the rapprochement in the mind of the General was intended in large part simply as a counter to, or a dilution of, NATO, as well as an instrument of French primacy on the Continent. Germany's participation in the General's plans thereupon became less enthusiastic. To the extent to which the French plans for Germany tended to cut across the NATO military commitments, they naturally also ran counter to the interests of all the NATO Allies. Inevitably a contest developed among the Allies for the adherence of Germany to opposing concepts in the Alliance—a sort of struggle for the soul of Faust, which was good neither for the Alliance nor for Germany. All are aware of the importance of Germany and the problems of the German settlement which in the not distant future we shall have to face. These problems will far transcend the question of how French troops should be stationed in Germany or the positioning of Allied troops elsewhere in Europe. The question of German reunification, and the location and defense of the Eastern boundaries and their stability, as well as new economic adjustments, are examples of the long-range problems on which a separatist approach would be unwise, if not disastrous.

In replying to General de Gaulle's letter of March 7, 1966, stating the intention of France to withdraw from the NATO structure, the President of the United States replied that the French position raised grave questions regarding the whole relationship between the responsibilities and the benefits of the Alliance. This is a serious statement and it indicates that the time may have come when, freed from any anachronisms that earlier experience and purely historical approaches may have tended to perpetuate, we must reappraise our interests in Europe. Our interests have to be reappraised also in the light of the new uncertainties which the French position has injected into the whole Western position of defense. It is difficult to avoid the conclusion that the French attitude constitutes a direct attack on the underlying basis for the Alliance itself, since the attempted distinction between the Alliance and NATO, on which the French communications place such stress, is really not convincing. The fact that the NATO Treaty antedated the agreements which added to its convincing character—agreements and resolutions to which France subscribed—is neither a legal nor a moral basis for the attempted distinction. Indeed, the stated reasons for the French disavowal of commitments of what is termed the "Organization" in distinction to the Treaty itself, as given in the memorandum accompanying the March 7 letter of General de Gaulle, can be addressed in the main to the validity of the Alliance itself. Perhaps this gave rise to a comment made by René Pleven or one of his colleagues in the recent debate in the Chamber that this was, at least, a legal separation and a legal separation usually, in the experience of the speaker, led to divorce. The reasons given, as reported in the *New York Times*, are as follows:

> First: The threat to Europe which produced the Atlantic Treaty has no longer the same "immediate and menacing character";
> Second: France now has a nuclear capacity that "naturally" cannot be integrated. The argument here appears to be that since "integration" is an aspect of NATO and French nuclear forces are non-integrable, it is anomalous to be thinking of "integration" in respect of any French forces;
> Third: A nuclear balance now exists between the Soviet Union and the United States—this is simply stated as a fact as justification for the French position; the reasoning is not set out but it can be conjectured;
> Fourth: Europe is no longer the center of international crises—Asia is, and the majority of NATO nations are not involved there.

If these reasons are valid, do they not indeed go to the heart of the Alliance, as President Johnson has suggested, and not merely to what General de Gaulle refers to as the "Organization"? The question is particularly pertinent since General de Gaulle has declared that no profit was to be derived from discussing any modification of NATO.

Let us consider the reasons given in their order. One can perhaps readily agree that for the time being, and, perhaps, for the foreseeable future, the pressures and strains on Western Europe will be less than they were when Stalin's postwar intentions first became manifest. The Soviet Union's differences with Red China, the added assertiveness of some of the satellites, the confrontation over Cuba, the existence of the Berlin Wall, the general well-being of the Continent and some moderation of the flow of polemics, all seem to suggest a less aggressive and less adventurous attitude on the part of the Soviet Union in regard to Europe. But we can well be reminded, without being alarmed, that Berlin is still invested, that scores of Russian divisions are still mobilized to the West, and that Soviet objectives in respect of Western Europe still persist in the absence of any tangible evidence of their abandonment. The existence of the Sino-Soviet schism, moreover, does not point exclusively in the direction of a pacific policy on the part of the Soviet Union. The latter is in a position, well known in history, where the leader of a radical movement finds his flank threatened on the left. A certain dynamism inevitably attaches to the extreme left and a threat to its loyalty usually produces reactions disturbing to the leader. The Soviet Union is charged by Red China throughout the world with being soft on imperialism and weak on classic Marxist-Leninist doctrines. Though there seems to be no present disposition on the part of Moscow to institute new adventures in the West, and though the Soviet Union is vexed by this challenge to its leadership, Moscow, it must be recalled, has not yet made its choice. Till that time comes the Soviet Union may be inclined to attempt diversions, if only to respond to the criticisms from Peking and their impact on the rest of the Communist World. The boldness of the Soviet attempt to implant intermediate-range missiles on the island of Cuba indicated, too recently for comfort, a willingness on the part of the Soviet Union to take great risks to advance its dominance in Europe, for it is clear to all who were aware of the facts that the Cuban episode had a direct bearing on the Soviet nuclear threat to Western Europe.

Berlin has not lost its essentially vulnerable position—the Wall is still up. One could readily imagine new pressures being applied there. All this would seem to point to the advisability of maintaining a deterrent which has thus far been successful rather than to urge steps which would encourage new threats.

The second reason given by General de Gaulle for the need to disavow the present form of NATO was that "naturally" France's nuclear capacity could not be "integrated." It may be asked, in passing, why it could not be integrated, or at least integrated in part (all significant United States nuclear power on the Continent is integrated, for example). It might well be more effective as a significant deterrent if France's nuclear strength were integrated. But assuming the *force de frappe* is not integrated and that France will never consent to its integration, it is well to consider what we mean by integration. Actually, the extent of integration of Allied forces now provided under NATO is generally misunderstood. Apart from certain air-defense forces which must be subject to constant alert, as Undersecretary Ball recently pointed out, no integrated commander, including the French general who holds the Central Allied Command, can order a single French soldier to move six inches forward or backward. What is meant by integration is agreed procedures, integrated headquarters, and agreed systems of command to take effect at the outbreak of hostilities, together with planning, target exercises, and some aspects of air defense. "Integration" was a response in large part to the charge of delayed intervention on the part of the United States in the case of prior danger. We can recall that the first World War was in real prospect of being lost when the United States, British, and French forces were integrated under Marshall Foch after the conference which took place, almost too late, at Doullens. Integration was also applied to the Allied forces in World War II and it materially contributed to the speed of victory. Integration, in short, was not an imposition on the part of the United States; it was a response to a demand or criticism on the part of Europe, including France, at the time the NATO discussions were taking place. But even if the French *force de frappe* was not integrated, it is difficult to see why the fundamental structure of the Alliance should be abandoned. France has had a nuclear capacity of sorts for some time and, but for some French balkiness in carrying out cooperative missions under NATO, no claim has been made, till now, that the separate nuclear capacity was inconsistent with NATO. No similar claim has been put forward by the British, who also have a separate nuclear capacity. In passing, another consideration might be pointed out. One of the dangers arising from France's assertion of a special position in Europe is the emphasis which is placed on the reason for it, namely, France's independent possession of the nuclear weapons. If the independent *force de frappe* entitles France to a position of greater dignity and prestige and if from its possession the stature of France in Europe is greatly enhanced, why, it may be argued, is its possession not essential for other European nonnuclear powers, including a power entirely competent to create a capacity, such as Germany? The French position becomes a really dangerous argument for proliferation of nuclear weapons.

The third reason given by General de Gaulle is the existence of a nuclear balance between the Soviet Union and the United States replacing the American nuclear monopoly. Here the reasoning is obscure or not clearly stated. Could it not be justly argued that during the period of the American nuclear monopoly there was little need for NATO and that now, when a delicate balance of nuclear strength exists between the Soviet Union and the United States, an effective NATO is all the more necessary? With the Soviet Union armed with nuclear weapons and announcing new developments in nuclear capacity and defense from month to month, it is difficult to see how it can be cogently maintained that less need for collective security exists now.

What General de Gaulle is probably getting at, without stating it too explicitly, is that Europe cannot rely on an American nuclear response, since the Russian nuclear potential would deter any such response. It is a repetition of the thought that the United States would not risk the destruction of its cities for the safety of Europe. In reply one can only repeat that the integration of American troops in a European defense system is about the best earnest one nation can give another of the reliability of its commitments. But, again, if the argument has any validity does it not go to the justification for any Alliance at all?

The final reason given for the abandonment of NATO is a corollary of the foregoing. It is that the dimension of the Soviet threat to Western Europe has lessened and that other parts of the world, in which Europe has little interest, have become more dangerous. It is argued that NATO was erected to take care of and to offset the Soviet threat in Europe and that the European members of NATO are not involved in conflicts outside of Europe. The implication is then drawn that European members of NATO may be embarrassed because other members of NATO have interests to protect and are involved in non-European areas. It is summed up in the French memorandum as follows: "International crises no longer center in Europe, but in Asia, and the majority of NATO countries are not involved in Asia."

The thought was repeated not long ago in the French Chamber when M. Pompidou referred to the fact that during the Cuban crisis the American air forces were on the alert in France.

Without accepting at face value the rather ambitious Chinese concept of a "rural" (that is, Asian, African, and South American) attack on the "city" areas (that is, Europe and the North Atlantic powers) through the activities of national liberation fronts, it would appear that whatever form and from whatever source attacks on Europe may be delivered, a united European or Atlantic policy to meet them would be appropriate. NATO was not formed to protect Berlin alone; it was not formed solely to protect Europe from the Soviet Union. It was designed to build a structure on which, with the defense of the West secure, a solid cohesive basis could be laid for long-range discussion and, if possible, settlement of all the major problems affecting the Atlantic world and the preservation of peace.

It has become the essence of the Red Chinese doctrine that Soviet Communism failed in Berlin and failed in Greece and it was unable to dominate the Western European peninsula. The Chinese contention is that now the Soviet Union should stand aside and allow new forces and new techniques to bring Europe and the "imperialistic" countries of the West under Communist influence. The target is still the North Atlantic, even though the attacks may not come over the parapets of Berlin. If the explosion comes in Asia, is it not just as important that policies successfully evolved in the North Atlantic Treaty be preserved to cope with such threats as well?

Certainly it seems shortsighted to argue that the areas in which the explosions are occurring in this foreshortened world are of no interest to Europe and concern only the non-European members of NATO. It is not suggested that NATO and its commitments be extended to include Southeast Asia, but the relation of NATO to Southeast Asia should not be overlooked. The fact that explosions have ceased or have moderated in the NATO area and have erupted elsewhere has certainly been due in large part to the convincing aspect of NATO in regard to Europe. The logic which would strike it down because dangers averted in Europe by reason of NATO have arisen in other sections is difficult to follow.

The problems created by the emergence of the underdeveloped countries are as acute as ever. The only nations which can hope to render effective assistance to the "have not" nations are the "have" nations. Generally speaking, these are the NATO countries. Certainly one of the major preoccupations of the nations constituting the NATO organization should be the economic problems of the underdeveloped nations and their peoples. To be sure, the NATO nations are faced with different problems. Some go far beyond those which confronted them when NATO was formed, but it is apparent that neither the defense needs of the area nor the wider opportunities or responsibilities of the NATO nations have thus far been fully achieved. Indeed, when one considers impending problems such as the future of Germany, the need for disarmament and arms control, the situation of the underdeveloped countries—problems which deeply affect all the NATO members—a plethora of exigencies appears, exigencies which require greater, rather than lesser, cohesion in the Alliance.

It is most interesting that George Washington in 1793 took the position that Europe, with its problems and controversies and its distant location, could be only an embarrassment to the United States. Today France seems to be taking the same view of America's situation, ignoring the fact that Europe's problems, for good or ill, with the foreshortening of the world have become the serious concern of the United States and of a good part of the other non-European world. To suggest that the problems of the American continent are of no concern to Europe, after Europe has had to depend on outside strength to preserve itself twice in the present century, is as anachronistic as Washington's policy of 1793 in relation to the present state of the world. But it is interesting to see how American and French attitudes have come around, full circle.

So much for the need of an integrated and cohesive Alliance to deal with defense and other exacting problems affecting the interest of the Atlantic nations. The emphasis which General de Gaulle has placed on the need for what he terms flexible national positions is disquieting. Nationalism breeds nationalism, and it is an incongruity to claim that modern conditions require a return to nationalism as distinguished from collective action. It would be discouraging indeed if, after the world's recent experience with major wars and in the face of the implications of nuclear armament, the Atlantic nations felt that they had no alternative but to return to nationalism in their attempt to avert further international violence. Would we not then be back to the unproductive welter of alliances and axes of the pre-1914 and pre-1939 eras which actually proved to be provocative of war rather than deterrent to it?

The suggestion is made, in some quarters, that if this major effort after World War II to preserve the peace in Europe collapsed, the United States would be tempted to return to its position of traditional isolationism or neutralism. Few seriously believe that the United States can return to isolationism, even if some people in this country nostalgically wish it. What might well develop, however, in the face of continued frustrations, would be a tendency on the part of the United States to go it alone, so to speak; to move toward what some writers call bipolarism.

Some do favor a direct Washington-Moscow approach, discarding our concentration on attempts to maintain a rather complex Western Alliance. Others, it is pointed out, can call at Moscow with at least as much to talk about as France can offer. There has been pressure to reach an agreement with the Soviet Union on the problem of nuclear proliferation, even at some risk to the Alliance. The United States and the U.S.S.R. have a common interest in the nonproliferation of nuclear weapons. The United States and the Soviet Union have incomparably the greatest accumulation of nuclear weapons and the greatest nuclear capacity of all the nations. Would it not be reasonable to assume that if the seeds of disintegration are sown in the Atlantic Alliance the United States might seek the simpler form of an understanding with the Soviet Union? Some argue that moving in this direction provides as great a hope of preserving the peace as is found in clinging to a patchwork NATO of which France is no longer a part. Stalin, and to a measurable extent, Khrushchev, had in mind just such bipolar arrangements with the United States, and neither could understand the policy of the United States which favored a united Europe and unprecedented efforts to rebuild its strength.

Then there is the problem of Germany. It is unlikely that the Germans will be disposed to accept the exclusive agency of France to effect an understanding with the Soviet Union for the unification of Germany or to act as arbiter between the East and the West. It has already been suggested that the French withdrawal from NATO seems to give the Germans an increased importance in the Alliance and in Europe. It is conceivable that Germany might also achieve a more important role in respect to the Soviet Union. The Soviet Union has been remarkably sensitive and perceptive in regard to the situs of power. In a fragmented Europe the Russians might well gravitate in their dealings toward Germany rather than France. They have done it before.

All these considerations, some remote and others not so remote, are bound to be stimulated by the French action. The profoundly disturbing fact is that the philosophy of the General's *démarche,* if followed, would have the effect of reinfecting Europe with nationalism.

It will not be a simple matter in the face of French opposition to marshal the high order of statesmanship required to preserve the reality of European collective security of which NATO was both the symbol and the guarantee. Certainly, it will be difficult, if not impossible, to accomplish without a very firm determination and a sustained effort on the part of all the remaining NATO members.

The question has to be posed as to whether it is worth the effort: Is it practical to maintain a convincing Alliance structure partly integrated and partly independent?

When General de Gaulle withdrew his Mediterranean naval units from NATO the question arose as to whether France would withdraw also its ground and air units. Few doubted that General de Gaulle wished to do so, but the leverage which the presence of French troops in Germany would give France in future political determinations was so great it was believed that he would hesitate to withdraw them. Now the withdrawal from NATO Command has been announced for July 1. If after this separation French troops still remain in Germany, their military purpose is substantially overweighed by the political significance of their continued presence. Serious military problems, of course, are presented. Quite apart from the danger to the remaining integrated forces in the event of trouble, through an uncertain French flank, deep psychological and political questions may well flow from such a situation. A special independent national position for the French troops in Germany is not only harmful to the concept of integration; it is disruptive of the effort to unite Western Europe and is poorly designed to lessen the growth of German nationalism. A special position for the French troops in Germany after France has declared that her sovereignty would be impaired by the presence of NATO troops in France would mean that while thirteen countries are treating Germany on the basis of equality, one country would be insisting on a discriminatory position for Germany. Even if the Germans for their own reasons agreed to this today, a dangerous seed of nationalism will have been planted for the future. In the light of history it is not a satisfactory answer to suggest that in such case the other powers could restrain Germany.

The question posed above, that is, whether the effort to maintain NATO partly integrated and partly nonintegrated is practical and worthwhile, is not an easy one to answer. One who participated to a degree in creating the structure and who was aware of the intention of the creators of NATO to generate new, far-reaching, and constructive concepts for the preservation of peace in a nuclear world, accepts the imminent changes reluctantly. Because the advantages to be gained from such concepts are so far-reaching and the alternatives are so doubtful, if not dangerous, one must consider the effort to preserve the structure in generally the form which we now have it to be eminently worth while; one must consider that effort an imperative for the statesmen of the Alliance.

It is not solely because Europe and its destiny remain a matter of deep concern and interest to the United States that this effort must be made. What is really involved is the preservation of the peace in a nuclear-powered world. It is this concern which transcends the interests of France, of Europe, and of the United States. Merely to return to a state of national "flexibilities" with their nineteenth-century diplomatic techniques is simply not good enough for the preservation of peace today. They were inadequate in the days of conventional warfare; they are less adequate now.

It is fanciful to suppose that any one nation possesses the key to the preservation of the peace or the eventual unification of Germany. Certainly nothing suggests that France, apart from the other members of the Alliance, possesses either the genius or the strength to be the arbiter on whose determinations peace can depend. On the other hand, France can make invaluable contributions, some which no other nation can match, to the solution of some of our common international problems. France, by her geographical position, her history, and her culture, is eminently entitled to a dignified and important role in any Western defense system, but her role is bound to be less significant and less helpful outside the Alliance than in it.

"National flexibilities" have led to disaster in the past. In the sense that this term is used by General de Gaulle, they could, and in all probability would, lead to the proliferation of nuclear weapons. The emphasis on nationalism and the disintegration of the NATO structure could well lead to the reëmergence of Germany as a nonintegrated, independently moving power whose separate actions would result in an uncertain and diverse Western position on the vital problems of the future.

It would be a mistake not to realize that to preserve a convincing NATO structure now requires strong emergency treatment. The Allies cannot simply deplore the present situation and stand still, for if they do NATO and the basic concepts and guarantees it represents will fall to pieces with consequences profoundly detrimental to both the East and the West. It will require more this time than American leadership and resources to reëstablish the Alliance in convincing form if the French withdrawal is final. Europe with its renewed strength and independent status should be able, even without France, to muster sufficient strength of purpose to unite in its own defense. Proportionate to their interest and responsibilities the British, Italian, and German governments must display increased leadership and statesmanship in the vigorous maintenance and support of the Alliance. The prompt response of the fourteen nations, strongly reasserting their adherence to NATO and their faith in the organization, has already been an encouraging sign of renewed European determination and will. Washington can and must support that strength of purpose, even though it cannot supply it alone. Moscow has already expressed its satisfaction over the French defection and, as short-sighted as this may be in the Soviet Union's long-range interest, one can expect that Moscow will do its best to discourage any further steps to preserve European unity and strength. What the United States can do at this juncture is to give assurance by act and deed of its determination to continue to align itself with a united European defense system built around willing partners in such a manner as always to have available a place of dignity and equality for France in that system.

France maintains that her action is in keeping with the passage of time, that her approach is modern and consistent with the strength and dignity of France. Actually, it follows a very ancient pattern. Let us hope that the statesmen of the Old World and of the New can chart a course which will avoid the consequences which have heretofore attended the operation of that ancient and dangerous pattern.

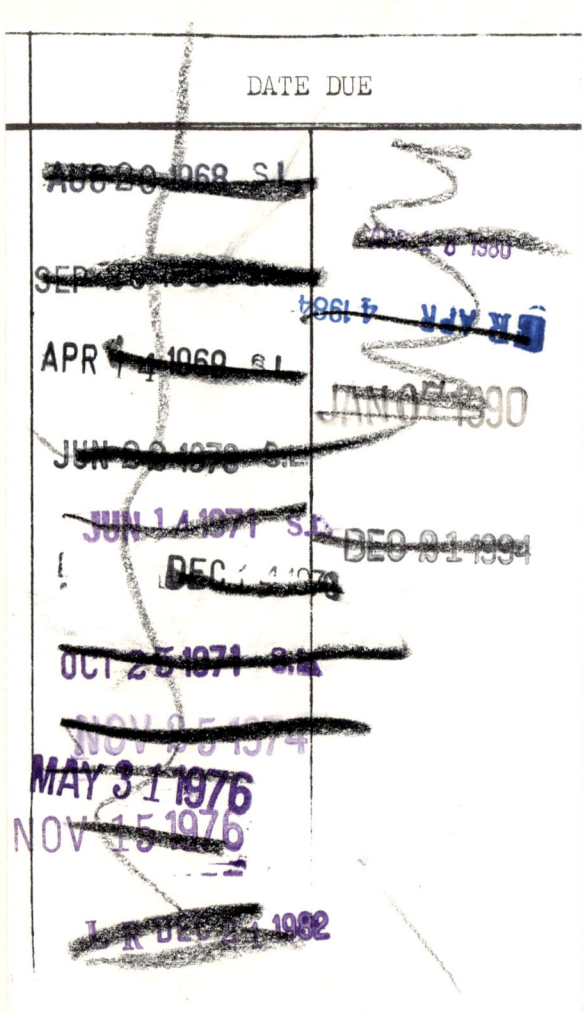